ENGLISH
LANGUAGE ARTS

Library of Congress Cataloging-in-Publication Data is available.

ISBN 978-0-7611-6091-5

Illustrator Kevin Jay Stanton
Series Designer Tim Hall   Designer Abby Dening
Editors Nathalie Le Du, Daniel Nayeri   Production Editor Jessica Rozler
Production Manager Julie Primavera
Concept by Raquel Jaramillo

Workman books are available at special discounts when purchased in bulk for premiums and sales promotions as well as for fund-raising or educational use. Special editions or book excerpts also can be created to specification. For details, contact the Special Sales Director at the address below, or send an email to specialmarkets@workman.com.

Workman Publishing Co., Inc.
225 Varick Street
New York, NY 10014-4381
workman.com

Printed in China

First printing August 2016
10 9 8 7 6 5 4

EVERYTHING YOU NEED TO ACE ENGLISH LANGUAGE ARTS IN ONE BIG FAT NOTEBOOK

Borrowed from the smartest kid in class
Double-checked by Jen Haberling

WORKMAN PUBLISHING
NEW YORK

EVERYTHING YOU NEED TO KNOW TO ACE

ENGLISH LANGUAGE ARTS

HI!

These are the notes from my English Language Arts class. Oh, who am I? Well, some people said I was the smartest kid in class.

I wrote everything you need to ace **ENGLISH**, from GREEK ROOTS to FICTION WRITING, and only the really important stuff in between—you know, the stuff that's usually on the test!

I tried to keep everything organized, so I almost always:

- Highlight vocabulary words in **YELLOW**.
- Color in definitions in green highlighter.
- Use BLUE PEN for important people, places, dates, and terms.
- Doodle a pretty sweet Alice and whatnot to visually show the big ideas.

AGREED!

If you're not loving your textbook and you're not so great at taking notes in class, this notebook will help. It hits all the major points. (But if your teacher spends a whole class talking about something that's not covered, go ahead and write that down for yourself.)

ZZZ...WHAT?

Now that I've aced English, this notebook is **YOURS**. I'm done with it, so this notebook's purpose in life is to help **YOU** learn and remember just what you need to ace **YOUR** English Language Arts class.

CONTENTS

Unit 1

GRAMMAR

GRAMMAR is the structure of a language—not what words mean, but the way words fit together: how the words in a sentence are arranged and the rules that explain how words get used. Think about grammar as if you're an architect—you need the right foundation and beams to hold up a building. Once that structure is strong, you can build anything!

Chapter 1

PHRASES
and
CLAUSES

PHRASES

A phrase is a group of words that acts as a single part of speech. A phrase can act like any part of speech, such as a noun, adjective, adverb, or **PREPOSITION**. A phrase never includes the subject of the sentence acting through a verb.

PREPOSITION
a word or group of words that shows direction, location, or time, or introduces an object

---

EXAMPLES:

GROUP OF WORDS ACTING LIKE A NOUN

Martinique's favorite sweater was hanging from the line.

Saskia found the sunset to be heart-stoppingly beautiful.

GROUP OF WORDS ACTING LIKE AN ADJECTIVE

GROUP OF WORDS ACTING LIKE AN ADVERB

Before class, I crammed for the test.

Percy took his pet lizard into the house.

GROUP OF WORDS ACTING LIKE A PREPOSITION

TYPES of PHRASES

A phrase can act as any part of speech, such as:

NOUN   **VERB**

ADVERB   **ADJECTIVE**

Noun Phrases

A NOUN PHRASE is a phrase that acts like a noun.

> **NOUN**
> a word that identifies a person, place, or thing

EXAMPLE:

The royal chef baked approximately 24 pies.

WORKS TOGETHER AS A NOUN

Verb Phrases

A VERB PHRASE is a phrase that acts like a verb.

EXAMPLE:

These strange rocks <u>may be worth</u> a fortune.

↑ WORKS TOGETHER AS A VERB

Adverb Phrases

An ADVERB PHRASE is a phrase that acts like an adverb.

EXAMPLE:

She moved through the library <u>like a spy through an enemy's headquarters.</u>

↑ WORKS TOGETHER AS AN ADVERB

Adjective Phrases

An ADJECTIVE PHRASE is a phrase that acts like an adjective.

EXAMPLE:

The crowd was <u>far more excited</u> now than during the first half of the game.

↑ WORKS TOGETHER AS AN ADJECTIVE

CLAUSES

A **CLAUSE** is a group of words that includes at least a subject and a verb. A clause always contains a subject that acts through a verb.

HOW TO TELL
CLAUSES AND PHRASES APART

* A phrase doesn't have a subject that acts through a verb.

* A clause DOES have a subject that acts through a verb.

EXAMPLES:

PHRASE	CLAUSE
In the nick of time	before the summer ended
NO VERB, SO IT'S A PHRASE	THE "SUMMER" IS DOING SOMETHING— IT'S ENDING—SO IT'S A CLAUSE.
Tripping merrily along	Because the wolf hid out in the forest
NO SUBJECT, SO IT'S A PHRASE	THERE IS A SUBJECT DOING SOMETHING—THE WOLF IS HIDING—SO IT'S A CLAUSE.

Clauses make up a pretty wide category! But they are categorized into two groups to help us work with them.

Independent Clauses

INDEPENDENT CLAUSES are clauses that can stand alone.

EXAMPLE:

I went to the bonfire after the game.

"I went to the bonfire" could be a stand-alone sentence, and thus it is an independent clause.

Dependent Clauses

DEPENDENT CLAUSES are clauses that can't stand alone.

EXAMPLE:

When the circus gets to town, we'll go to see the elephants.

"WHEN THE CIRCUS GETS TO TOWN" COULD NOT BE A FULL SENTENCE.

TYPES OF DEPENDENT CLAUSES

There are three types of dependent clauses:

NOUN CLAUSE: a dependent clause that acts like a noun

A CLAUSE NEVER ACTS LIKE A VERB.

ADJECTIVE CLAUSE: a dependent clause that acts like an adjective

ADVERB CLAUSE: a dependent clause that acts like an adverb

EXAMPLES:

ACTS LIKE A NOUN

I don't know <u>why he did that</u>.

He really loved the jacket <u>that she sold him</u>.

MODIFIES THE NOUN, SO IT ACTS LIKE AN ADJECTIVE

All the kids tried to eat their Popsicles <u>before they melted in the hot sun</u>.

MODIFIES THE VERB, SO IT ACTS LIKE AN ADVERB

Misplaced Modifiers

A misplaced modifier is a phrase or a clause in the wrong place, so no one knows what the phrase or clause is supposed to modify.

EXAMPLE:

THE MEAT LOAF WAS COMING IN THE DOOR?!

Greta smelled the meat loaf <u>coming in the house</u> for dinner.

THAT'S WEIRD ... AND PROBABLY DELICIOUS.

How to fix it: Make sure modifiers are close to what they modify—and not near anything else they might modify—so no one gets confused.

EXAMPLE:

Coming in the house for dinner, Greta smelled the meat loaf.

Greta is the subject coming in the house, so the phrase should be closer to her than to the meat loaf. Now it's too far from the meat loaf for anyone to get confused.

Dangling Modifiers

A dangling modifier is a phrase or a clause that modifies something that is not even in the sentence. Again, no one has a clue what the phrase or clause is supposed to modify.

EXAMPLE:

Excited for the first game of the season, Javi's hockey skates sat in the front hall, ready to be worn.

← BUT HOCKEY SKATES CAN'T BE EXCITED!

How to fix it: Make sure the thing a phrase modifies is actually in the sentence.

EXAMPLE:

Excited for the first game of the season, Javi kept his hockey skates in the front hall, ready to be worn.

JAVI'S SKATES CAN'T GET EXCITED . . . BUT ← JAVI CAN.

COMPOUND AND COMPLEX SENTENCES

> Don't forget that a SIMPLE SENTENCE:
> * contains a subject and a verb
> * contains a complete idea

Phrases and clauses can be added to simple sentences in many ways.

EXAMPLES:

She walked.

SUBJECT — VERB

COMPLETE THOUGHT (THEREFORE, A SIMPLE SENTENCE)

She walked in the door.

PLUS A PHRASE

Phrases and clauses can also create
COMPOUND and COMPLEX SENTENCES.

> A COMPOUND SENTENCE contains:
> * two or more independent clauses (each clause could be its own sentence)
>
> A COMPLEX SENTENCE contains:
> * an independent clause and one (or more) dependent clauses

The clauses in a compound or complex sentence are connected by a COORDINATING CONJUNCTION, which is a **CONJUNCTION** that appears between words, phrases, or clauses that are grammatically similar or have equal importance in the sentence. Some conjunctions are **FOR, AND, NOR, BUT, OR, YET**, and **SO**.

> **CONJUNCTION**
> a word that connects clauses or sentences

Want to remember coordinating conjunctions? Just remember **FANBOYS**:

For
And
Nor
But
Or
Yet
So

EXAMPLE: a compound sentence:

INDEPENDENT CLAUSE

The girl walked in the door, (and) her mother gave her a
huge hug.

INDEPENDENT CLAUSE

COORDINATING CONJUNCTION

IF YOU LIKE FORMULAS,
TRY THINKING OF IT LIKE THIS:

Independent Clause + Coordinating Conjunction +
Independent Clause = Compound Sentence

Or IC+CC+IC = Compound Sentence

Sometimes the clauses in a complex sentence are connected by a SUBORDINATING CONJUNCTION. A subordinating conjunction (also known as a subordinate conjunction) links a dependent clause to an independent clause. So, what's the difference between subordinating and coordinating conjunctions? While coordinating conjunctions join clauses of equal importance, subordinating conjunctions make one clause subordinate to (or dependent on) the other.

SOME COMMON SUBORDINATING CONJUNCTIONS ARE:
after, although, as, because, before, even though, every time, if, in case, now that, once, since, though, unless, until, when, whenever, whether or not, while.

Try thinking of it like this: The dependent clause is subordinate to the independent clause—it serves the independent clause's meaning.

Often, a subordinating clause will show a time, place, or cause and effect relationship.

EXAMPLE: INDEPENDENT CLAUSE

Her mother gave her a huge smile, (because) she had gotten there just in time.

DEPENDENT CLAUSE

SUBORDINATING CONJUNCTION THAT GIVES A REASON

EXAMPLE: DEPENDENT CLAUSE THAT SHOWS TIME

Once I cleaned my room, I was allowed to go to the movies.

INDEPENDENT CLAUSE

Many of the same conjunctions are subordinate and coordinating conjunctions—so the important thing to remember is simply that you need conjunctions to connect independent and dependent clauses.

Compound Complex Sentences

A COMPOUND COMPLEX SENTENCE is made of two (or more) independent clauses and one (or more) dependent clauses.

EXAMPLE: DEPENDENT CLAUSE   INDEPENDENT CLAUSE

Because she had gotten there just in time, she was able to help her mother finish cooking dinner, so they were also able to play a quick game together.

INDEPENDENT CLAUSE

COORDINATING CONJUNCTION

EXAMPLE:

INDEPENDENT CLAUSE   SUBORDINATE CONJUNCTION   DEPENDENT CLAUSE

It didn't take me long to get to school, when I borrowed my brother's flying horse, and I soared over the traffic.

COORDINATING CONJUNCTION   INDEPENDENT CLAUSE

1. Does a phrase contain a subject that acts through a verb?

2. What is missing from a sentence with a dangling modifier?

3. Is "but" a coordinating or a subordinating conjunction?

4. Rewrite this sentence so the modifier is clear:
   Before they melted the kids decorated the snowmen.

5. Can a dependent clause work as its own sentence?

6. State all the coordinating conjunctions.

7. How many independent clauses does a simple sentence have?

8. What type of sentence has a dependent clause—a compound sentence or a complex sentence?

9. What must any clause contain?

10. Which of these is NOT a kind of clause?

Adverb clause, verb clause, noun clause, adjective clause

CHECK YOUR ANSWERS

1. No

2. A dangling modifier is missing the thing that the modifier describes (sometimes the subject of the sentence).

3. "But" is a coordinating conjunction.

4. The kids decorated the snowmen before they melted.

5. No

6. For, and, nor, but, or, yet, so (Just remember FANBOYS!)

7. One

8. A complex sentence

9. A subject that acts through a verb

10. A verb clause is not a kind of clause.

Chapter 2

SUBJECTIVE, OBJECTIVE, and POSSESSIVE PRONOUNS

PRONOUNS

A **PRONOUN** is a word that takes the place of a noun (person, place, or thing).

★ ★ ★

Mindy ran for class president. / She ran for class president. "SHE" TAKES THE PLACE OF "MINDY."

The soccer players celebrated. / They celebrated.

The Eiffel Tower lit up the night sky. / It lit up the night sky.

Subjective Pronouns

SUBJECTIVE PRONOUNS are pronouns that take the place of the subject of a sentence.

> The **SUBJECT OF A SENTENCE** is:
> The thing that **DOES** something in a sentence
> OR
> The thing that **IS** something in a sentence
>
> EXAMPLES:
>
> **DOES**: Terry rides his bike.
> ↳ SUBJECT
>
> **IS**: The tree is the tallest in the forest.
> SUBJECT ↗

Some subjective pronouns are I, YOU, HE, SHE, IT, WE, THEY, WHAT, and WHO.

EXAMPLES:

I climbed a mountain.

You gave me an apple.

I DID IT!

YOU → ME

He
~~Prashant~~ went to the store.

She
~~Genevieve~~ won the swimming competition.

<u>It</u> was raining.

We
~~Cameron and I~~ danced all night.

They
~~Tae and Phil~~ came from the city.

<u>What</u> happened?

<u>Who</u> did this?

Objective Pronouns

An OBJECTIVE PRONOUN is a pronoun that takes the place of the object of a sentence.

The **OBJECT OF A SENTENCE**
is the thing that something **HAPPENS TO**
in a sentence.

EXAMPLES:

Sasha hit the <u>ball</u>.
↖ OBJECT
Jeremy carried the <u>bouquet of flowers</u>.
OBJECT ↗

Some objective pronouns are **ME, YOU, HIM, HER, IT, US, THEM, WHOM**, and **THAT**.

EXAMPLES:

HELP!

The pile of blankets fell on <u>me</u>.

I waved to <u>you</u>.

Please tell Jack I want to see ~~Jack~~ him

We went over to help ~~Kim.~~ her

No one could believe ~~the story.~~ it

He took ~~Tim and me~~ to the park. us

She explained the history to ~~the group of tourists.~~ them

He was a friend <u>whom</u> she met in Kenya.

I need to move ~~the tree.~~ that

Possessive Pronouns

POSSESSIVE PRONOUNS show that something belongs to someone. Some possessive pronouns are **MINE, YOURS, HIS, HERS, OURS,** and **THEIRS.**

EXAMPLES:

The last piece of pizza is <u>mine</u>.

 I think this dirty sock is <u>yours</u>.

> "Yours" can be singular OR plural. We use it whether one person owns something or many people own it together.

David wanted everyone to know the new puppy was <u>his</u>.

 Maria's mother told her that one day the ring would be ~~Maria's~~ hers

Are these seats <u>ours</u>?

I'm sorry, this cake is ~~the Mitchells'~~ theirs

INAPPROPRIATE SHIFTS

WELL, THAT WAS INAPPROPRIATE!

An INAPPROPRIATE SHIFT is using the wrong pronoun to replace a noun. There are two kinds:

Inappropriate Shift #1: Wrong Number

A WRONG NUMBER is when the sentence has:

* a pronoun that should be plural replacing a noun that's **SINGULAR**
* a pronoun that should be singular replacing a noun that's **PLURAL**

> **PLURAL:** more than one
> **SINGULAR:** just one

EXAMPLES:

SINGULAR   PLURAL

Every time <u>I</u> go to the beach, <u>we</u> get a hot dog.   WRONG NUMBER

PLURAL   PLURAL

Every time <u>we</u> go to the beach, <u>we</u> get hot dogs.   NUMBERS MATCH: CORRECT!

SINGULAR   PLURAL

If <u>anyone</u> wants to come to the party, <u>they</u> need to reply to the invitation.   WRONG NUMBER

SINGULAR

If <u>anyone</u> wants to come to the party, <u>he or she</u> needs to reply to the invitation.   NUMBERS MATCH: CORRECT!

SINGULAR

Inappropriate Shift #2: Wrong Case

A WRONG CASE is when a sentence uses the wrong type of pronoun, such as incorrectly using an objective pronoun when the sentence calls for a subjective pronoun.

For example, it's possible to use both "**I**" and "**ME**" to write about myself. It's possible to use both "**HE**" and "**HIM**" to write about my dad. But they don't go in the same place in a sentence. "I" and "he" are subjective. They belong as the subject of a sentence. "Me" and "him" are objective. They belong as the object of a sentence.

EXAMPLES:

<u>Me</u> want an ice cream cone.   WRONG CASE

<u>I</u> want an ice cream cone.   CORRECT CASE

I'm going over to see <u>he</u>.   WRONG CASE

I'm going over to see <u>him</u>.   CORRECT CASE

OTHER PRONOUN PROBLEMS
Vague Pronouns

A VAGUE PRONOUN is where it's not clear what the pronoun is replacing. So everyone gets confused.

EXAMPLES:

Jared's brother wondered if <u>he</u> was fast enough to win the race.

WHO ARE YOU TALKING ABOUT?

Who is "he" in this sentence? Jared, or his brother? Nobody knows!

Abby wanted to get a new scooter because <u>it</u> was cool.

Is it cool to have the scooter? Or is the scooter cool? Nobody knows!

To fix a vague pronoun, be specific—make sure nobody can get confused by what you're saying.

EXAMPLES:

Jared's brother wondered if <u>Jared</u> was fast enough to win the race.

OR

Jared's brother wondered if <u>he himself</u> was fast enough to win the race.

Abby wanted to get a new scooter because <u>owning a new scooter</u> was cool.

OR

Abby wanted to get a new scooter because <u>the scooter</u> was cool.

Compound Pronouns

A COMPOUND PRONOUN is a combination of pronouns used as the subject or object of a sentence.

EXAMPLE:

"I made enough bracelets for <u>you and your friends</u>."

When we refer to ourselves alone, we usually use "I." We say, "I went to the store." We don't say, "Me went to the store." But when we add in another person, sometimes things get mixed up.

EXAMPLE:

 INCORRECT

"Me and Hannah went to the store."

To fix a compound pronoun, first take out the other person.

Me ~~and Hannah~~ went to the store.

You can see right away that's not correct, so change it to the proper case:

I went to the store.

Lastly, add the other person back in:

Hannah and I went to the store.

Works like magic! But how do we know to put "Hannah" first?

In general, when using compound pronouns, all pronouns except "I" come before the noun in the sentence.

EXAMPLE:

He and Sheryl read the same book.

PRONOUN   NOUN

The pronoun "he" is placed before the noun "Sheryl."
If the same sentence were written with the pronoun "I," we would put "I" last.

Sheryl and I read the same book.

AN EASY WAY TO REMEMBER THIS: THINK ABOUT YOUR MANNERS! ALWAYS PUT OTHERS BEFORE "I."

1. In the following sentence, is "they" subjective, objective, or possessive?

   They went to the movie.

2. Which sentence is correct?

   Bob and me met him.

   Bob and I met him.

3. What does a possessive pronoun do?

4. Change the object of this sentence to a pronoun:

   Jessica loved her new bike.

5. Correct this sentence:

   Each person must hang up their coat.

6. What does "plural" mean?

7. Rewrite this sentence two different ways, so there is no confusion about what it might mean:

   Jogen ran to the park because he loved it.

8. In the following sentence, is "us" subjective, objective, or possessive?

They finally let us in.

9. Correct this sentence:

That flag belongs to us, so it's mine.

10. There's an inappropriate shift in the following sentence. Is it a shift in number or in case?

If one of us wins the race, you can get a big medal at the finish line.

1. "They" is subjective.

2. Bob and I met him.

3. Shows ownership

4. Jessica loved it.

5. Each person must hang up his or her coat.
   Everyone must hang up their coat.

6. More than one

7. Jogen ran to the park because he loved to run.
   Jogen ran to the park because he loved the park.

8. Objective

9. That flag belongs to us, so it's ours.
   That flag belongs to me, so it's mine.

10. Case

Chapter 3

INTENSIVE PRONOUNS

INTENSIVE PRONOUNS

An **INTENSIVE PRONOUN** is a pronoun that emphasizes its antecedent. ←

> The word that a pronoun refers back to and replaces in a sentence

EXAMPLE:

(My brother) tied his shoes himself.

ANTECEDENT

INTENSIVE PRONOUN

I DID IT MYSELF!

Intensive pronouns always end with "self" or "selves."
Some intensive pronouns are **MYSELF, HIMSELF, HERSELF, YOURSELF, ITSELF, THEMSELVES, OURSELVES**, and **YOURSELVES**.

EXAMPLES:

I saw the aliens myself.

He pulled her out of the river himself.

Grandma will drive the car herself.

You need to clean your room yourself.

The band itself is amazing, even without the fancy costumes.

The cats turned the faucet on themselves.

We can carry our groceries ourselves.

You yourselves know what it's like to win a game.

Intensive and Reflexive Pronouns

An intensive pronoun can also be used as a **REFLEXIVE** pronoun, which refers to the subject of the sentence, clause, or phrase in which it stands.

> **REFLEXIVE**
> a word or phrase that refers back to itself

Huh? What's the difference? If you take a reflexive pronoun out of a sentence, it changes the meaning of the sentence.

EXAMPLE:

She made ~~herself~~ a green dress. ←

She made a green dress. ←

> The meaning is not the same. Now we don't know who will get to wear the dress!

If you take an intensive pronoun out of a sentence, the meaning stays the same.

EXAMPLE:

She ~~herself~~ made a green dress.

She made a green dress. ←

> The meaning is the same. We didn't lose any information.

33

Myself and Yourself

"Myself" and "yourself" get misused a lot, but intensive pronouns only belong in a sentence for one reason: to emphasize something. Otherwise, we should use the correct subjective, objective, or possessive pronoun.

"MYSELF" EXAMPLE:

Dan and myself will be leading the class.

Is this correct? We can double-check by taking "Dan" out to see how the sentence sounds.

This doesn't sound right.

Myself will be leading the class.

I will be leading the class.   Now it sounds good!

Let's add Dan back in.

Dan and I will be leading the class.

Now it's correct!

34

"YOURSELF" EXAMPLE:

Only your sister and yourself will take the bus.

What is the proper word here? What if we take out "your sister" and see how the sentence sounds?

This sounds wrong.

Yourself will take the bus.

You will take the bus.   Sounds better!

Now let's add "your sister" back in.

Only your sister and you will take the bus.   Now it's correct!

1. Which kind of pronoun can you remove from a sentence without changing the meaning of the sentence?

2. What two endings appear on all intensive pronouns?

3. What is the plural of "yourself"?

4. Which of these sentences is correct?

   Becca and myself will make the lemonade.

   Becca and I will make the lemonade.

   Becca and me will make the lemonade.

5. Add an intensive pronoun to this sentence:

   She studied the mitochondria.

6. This sentence has an inappropriate shift. Is it a problem with case or a problem with number?

   Students yourselves need to pick up the test.

7. Rewrite the sentence above with the proper intensive pronoun.

8. Fill in the blank:

You can finish the science experiment _____.

9. In the following sentence, is "ourselves" reflexive or intensive?

Terence and I bought ourselves gliders at the fair.

10. Fill in the blank:

I _____ don't have a problem with it.

CHECK YOUR ANSWERS

1. Intensive

2. Self or selves

3. Yourselves

4. Becca and I will make the lemonade.

5. She studied the mitochondria herself.
or
She herself studied the mitochondria.

6. Case

7. Students themselves need to pick up the test.

8. Yourself

9. Reflexive

10. Myself

Chapter 4

VERBALS

VERBALS

A **VERBAL** is just a label for something that has to do with a verb. VERBAL PHRASES are phrases that begin with verbs. There are three types of verbal phrases:

- Gerunds
- Participles
- Infinitives

GERUNDS

A **GERUND** is a verb that turns into a noun. How? By adding "ing"!

LIKE GRAMMAR MAGIC!

EXAMPLES:

To run ⟶ running

To think ⟶ thinking

To play ⟶ playing

You can use a gerund the same way you use a noun—as the subject or the object of a sentence.

EXAMPLES:

Running made her feel better.

SUBJECT

She thought about running.

OBJECT

Gerund Phrases

A GERUND PHRASE is a phrase that begins with a gerund.

EXAMPLES:

Running around the park

Thinking of his friends

Playing basketball after dark

A gerund phrase still acts like a noun in a sentence.

EXAMPLE:

Running to the store gave her some time outside.

GERUND PHRASE ACTING AS A NOUN
AND SUBJECT OF THE SENTENCE

PARTICIPLES

A **PARTICIPLE** is a verb that turns into an adjective.

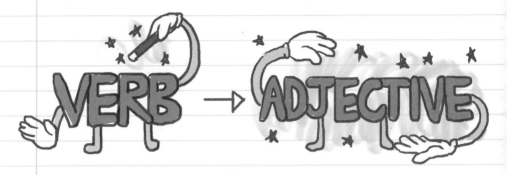

Past and Present Participles

PAST PARTICIPLE

* Usually ends in -n, -en, -t, -ed, -d
* Acts like an adjective

EXAMPLES:

THE PARTICIPLE MODIFIES "APPLE."

half-eaten apple

ruined castle

PRESENT PARTICIPLE

* Ends in -ing
* Used with another verb
* Acts like an adjective

EXAMPLES:

THE PARTICIPLE MODIFIES "SHE."

She was eating an apple.

They were ruining a castle.

How do you make a past participle? If it's a regular verb, just use normal past tense. You can use participles anywhere you use an adjective (to modify a noun).

EXAMPLES:

walk ⟶ walked

smile ⟶ smiled

dance ⟶ danced

If it's NOT a regular verb . . . there aren't any rules! Plan to learn them as you go.

EXAMPLES:

begin ⟶ begun

forgive ⟶ forgiven

sing ⟶ sung

Participle Phrases

A PARTICIPLE PHRASE is a phrase that begins with a participle.

EXAMPLES:

Listening to the rain

Forgotten for years

Dancing as if there were no tomorrow

A participle phrase still acts like an adjective in a sentence.

EXAMPLE:

PARTICIPLE PHRASE THAT MODIFIES "PRESTON"

Dancing as if there were no tomorrow, Preston accidentally fell off the end of the dock.

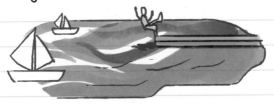

"RUNNING TO THE STORE"—is it a gerund or participle phrase? (Both end in –ing.)

The same phrase can be a gerund or a present participle, depending on how it is used in the sentence:

> GERUND = used as noun
> PRESENT PARTICIPLE = used as adjective

USED AS NOUN AND SUBJECT OF SENTENCE, THEREFORE A GERUND PHRASE

Running to the store gave Abby time to think things through.

Running to the store, Abby got caught in the rain.

ADJECTIVE THAT MODIFIES "ABBY," THEREFORE A PARTICIPLE PHRASE

INFINITIVES

An **INFINITIVE** is a verb phrase that almost always begins with "to" and ends with a verb.

{
To have
To talk
To explore

Infinitives can be used as nouns, adjectives, or adverbs.

EXAMPLES:

To walk was her greatest desire.

↖ SUBJECT OF SENTENCE AND ACTS LIKE A NOUN

The way to go is through the woods.

↖ MODIFIES "WAY," SO IT ACTS LIKE AN ADJECTIVE

He hoped to understand.

↑ EXPLAINS WHY HE HOPES, SO IT ACTS LIKE AN ADVERB

Infinitive Phrases

An INFINITIVE PHRASE is a phrase that begins with an infinitive.

EXAMPLES:

To hope for a better tomorrow
INFINITIVE

To forget all your fears
INFINITIVE

To walk into the sunset
INFINITIVE

Infinitive phrases also act like nouns, adjectives, or adverbs in a sentence.

EXAMPLES:

To walk across the state was her greatest desire.

INFINITIVE PHRASE THAT ACTS LIKE A NOUN AND SUBJECT OF SENTENCE

It was the fastest way to get from here to there.

INFINITIVE PHRASE THAT MODIFIES "WAY," SO IT'S ACTING LIKE AN ADJECTIVE

He hoped to understand what really happened all those years ago.

INFINITIVE PHRASE THAT EXPLAINS WHAT HE HOPES, SO IT'S ACTING LIKE AN ADVERB

CHECK YOUR KNOWLEDGE

1. Is a phrase that begins with "to" a gerund phrase? If not, what is it?

2. Does a past participle or a present participle end with "ing"?

3. What part of speech does a gerund act like?

4. What kind of phrase only acts as an adjective?

5. Is the underlined phrase a gerund phrase or a participle phrase?
   Singing in the shower was his favorite way to start the day.

6. What kind of verbal never ends with "ing"?

7. What three parts of speech can an infinitive act like?

8. Which part of speech does the underlined infinitive phrase act like?

She had always wished <u>to have a place of her own.</u>

9. What is the past participle of "write"?

10. What kind of phrase is underlined here?

<u>Singing her heart out,</u> Kamilah danced across the stage.

ANSWERS

CHECK YOUR ANSWERS

1. No, it's an infinitive phrase.

2. A present participle ends with "ing."

3. A gerund acts like a noun.

4. A participle phrase acts like an adjective.

5. A gerund phrase

6. An infinitive never ends with "ing."

7. An infinitive can act like a noun, adjective, or adverb.

8. An adverb

9. Written

10. A present participle phrase

Chapter 5

ACTIVE and PASSIVE VOICE and VERBS

VERBS: ACTIVE AND PASSIVE

A verb can be either active or passive. When a verb is ACTIVE, the subject of the sentence actually does something.

EXAMPLES:

Jessica <u>hit</u> the ball out of the park.

JESSICA DOES SOMETHING TO THE BALL—SHE HITS IT!

EXAMPLES:

Jose <u>sang</u> a song.

Jiang <u>performed</u> the new dance.

When a verb is PASSIVE, it means that something HAPPENS to the subject of the sentence.

EXAMPLES:

The ball <u>was hit</u> out of the park by Jessica.

HEY!!!

SOMETHING HAPPENED TO THE BALL—JESSICA HIT IT.

The song <u>was sung</u> by Jose.

The new dance <u>was performed</u> by Jiang.

When a verb in a sentence is an active verb, we say it's in the ACTIVE VOICE.

When a verb in a sentence is a passive verb, we say it's in the PASSIVE VOICE.

How to Make a Passive Verb

Active verbs are simple. We just use the basic form of the verb, in the proper tense.

EXAMPLES:

Past tense: Kate walked.

Present tense: Kate walks.

Future tense: Kate will walk.

To make a verb passive takes another step. We add some form of "to be" to the verb.

SUCH AS "IS," "WAS," OR "WILL BE"!

EXAMPLES:

Past tense: The dog <u>was</u> walked.

Present tense: The dog <u>is</u> walked.

Future tense: The dog <u>will be</u> walked.

Just add "to be" verbs to make a verb passive!

Active or Passive: What Should We Use?

Sometimes we have to use the passive voice. There may just be no other way to say something or emphasize something being acted upon. But in general, text sounds better when we use the active voice and active verbs. (Would you rather read about someone who sits around and just lets things happen to them, or would you rather read about someone who actually does stuff?)

EXAMPLES:

Jim jumped out of the plane.

The plane was jumped out of by Jim.

THE EMPHASIS IS ON THE PLANE— NOT JIM—THAT'S AWKWARD.

Usually, the active voice expresses the action more clearly and succinctly. Unintentional passive sentences are usually really awkward. So whenever you can, make sure your verbs are active, not passive!

Don't Shift! Keep Your Verbs and Voice Consistent

But whatever you do, just don't switch from active to passive voice in the same sentence.

EXAMPLE:

When Alice **pulled** the fire alarm, a loud ringing **was heard**.

ACTIVE! ←————— DOESN'T MATCH! —————→ PASSIVE!

If you begin in active voice, make sure all your verbs are active.

EXAMPLE:

When Alice **pulled** the fire alarm, the students **heard** a loud ringing.

ACTIVE! ←————— IT'S A MATCH! —————→ ACTIVE!

And if you begin in passive voice, make sure all your verbs stay passive.

EXAMPLE:

When the fire alarm was **pulled**, a loud ringing **was heard**.

PASSIVE! ←————— THEY MATCH! —————→ PASSIVE!

CHECK YOUR KNOWLEDGE

1. Which voice uses a form of the verb "to be," active or passive?

2. Is this sentence in active or passive voice?
   Jim ran a mile.

3. Which one of these sentences is in passive voice?
   Dara cleaned her room.
   The room was cleaned by Dara.

4. Whenever possible, which voice should we write in, active or passive?

5. If something happens to the subject in a sentence, is the sentence active or passive?

6. Are the two verbs in this sentence in the same voice?
   After Jeremy finished his dinner, he ate an entire bowl of raspberries.

7. Are the verbs in this sentence active or passive?
   As soon as the books were delivered, they were taken to the president.

8. Rewrite this active sentence as passive:

Janet ran the mile in under five minutes.

9. Rewrite this passive sentence as active:

The mill was closed by Mr. Turner after the price of cotton fell.

10. Correct this sentence so that both verbs are in the active voice:

After the men felled the tree, it was carried to town.

CHECK YOUR ANSWERS

1. Passive

2. Active

3. The room was cleaned by Dara.

4. Active

5. Passive

6. Yes

7. Passive

8. The mile was run by Janet in under five minutes.

9. Mr. Turner closed the mill after the price of cotton fell.

10. After the men felled the tree, they carried it to town.

Chapter 6

VERBS
and
MOOD

Did you know a verb could be in a mood? But the **MOOD** of a verb doesn't tell us how a verb feels; rather, it tells us how the person who is ACTING the verb feels.

MOODS of VERBS

The moods of a verb have completely different names than a person's mood.

HAPPY

SAD

GRUMPY

SLEEPY

NOT FEELING THAT. VERB

INDICATIVE VERBS are used when we state a fact.

EXAMPLES:

Past: I biked.

Present: I bike.

Future: I will bike.

IT'S TRUE—
I BIKE.

JUST THE FACTS!

IMPERATIVE VERBS are used when we tell someone what to do.

EXAMPLES:

<u>Get</u> out of bed!

<u>Open</u> the door!

UGH, STOP TELLING ME WHAT TO DO!

INTERROGATIVE VERBS
are used when we ask a question.

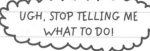

EXAMPLES:

<u>Will</u> we see a shooting star tonight?

<u>Will</u> you help me carry this puppy home?

CONDITIONAL VERBS are used when something else has to happen before the action described by the verb can occur.

EXAMPLES:

If you leave that cat alone with the tuna casserole, he <u>might</u> eat it.

He <u>would</u> look nice if he got a new hat.

SUBJUNCTIVE VERBS are used when we describe thoughts or wishes that might not come true.

EXAMPLES:

I <u>wish</u> I were ten feet tall.

I <u>suggest</u> you clean that up before your sister sees it.

Conditional and Subjunctive: What's the Difference?

Conditional and subjunctive verbs have something in common: They both express information about things that haven't happened—things that are imagined. So how do we tell them apart?

Conditional verbs are used to express things that WOULD happen, IF the circumstances were right.

Subjunctive verbs are rarely used, but when they are, they usually express things that probably could never happen.

CONDITIONAL   OR   SUBJUNCTIVE

EXAMPLE:

If Maurice threw the birdseed to the pigeons, the birds
would eat it.

CONDITIONAL VERB

Whether or not the birds eat is conditional—it all depends on
the old man throwing birdseed.

Subjunctive verbs are used to
describe things that might not
happen at all, like this:

EXAMPLE:

If you were a bird, you
would eat Maurice's birdseed.

SUBJUNCTIVE VERB

Subjunctive verbs are also used to describe things that will
definitely never happen.

EXAMPLE:

Maurice wished that he
would be able to ride a giant
pigeon to the moon and back.

SUBJUNCTIVE VERB

Maurice could never ride a pigeon, and yet these verbs allow
for a hypothetical situation.

Don't Be Moody!

It's no fun to be around someone whose mood is always changing. That's true for verbs, too. If a sentence starts in one mood, it shouldn't switch to another.

Switching from imperative (telling someone what to do) to indicative (stating the facts)

EXAMPLE:

Don't <u>forget</u> your hat, and you <u>should wear</u> shoes.

IMPERATIVE   INDICATIVE

The mood in the sentence shifted. To fix it, make both verbs imperative:

Don't <u>forget</u> your hat, and <u>wear</u> shoes.

Or make both verbs indicative:

You <u>should remember</u> your hat, and you <u>should wear</u> shoes.

COMMON MISTAKE #2

Switching from conditional or subjunctive (something that might or might not happen) to indicative (something that will)

EXAMPLE: SUBJUNCTIVE   INDICATIVE

If this rocket <u>could fly</u> into the past, it <u>will have</u> a hard time finding rocket fuel before rockets were invented.

To fix it, make both verbs subjunctive: SUBJUNCTIVE

If this rocket <u>could fly</u> into the past, it <u>would have</u> a hard time finding rocket fuel before rockets were invented.

1. If you want to tell someone what to do, what verb mood do you use?

2. What mood is this sentence in?
   Will you help me with this?

3. What is the indicative mood used for?

4. Which mood would you use if you wanted to write about a dream that you knew couldn't come true?

5. Is this sentence imperative or indicative?
   Get out of here!

6. If you wanted to tell your little brother how much trouble he'd be in if he ate the strawberries you'd been saving, what mood would you use?

7. Rewrite this sentence in the imperative mood:
   I would like you to let the dog in.

8. If you ask a question, what verb mood are you using?

9. Is this sentence conditional or subjunctive?

If I had elastic arms, I could pick the pears from the tree in my neighbor's yard.

10. This sentence contains a shift in mood. Rewrite it so that all the verbs are conditional:

I get a watermelon at the farm stand, and I will eat the whole thing.

ANSWERS

1. Imperative

2. Interrogative

3. Stating the facts

4. Subjunctive

5. Imperative

6. Conditional

7. Let the dog in.

8. Interrogative

9. Subjunctive

10. If I get a watermelon at the farm stand, I will eat the whole thing.

Chapter 7

DEFINING FROM CONTEXT

WHAT IS CONTEXT?

Have you ever heard your mom talking about someone? You've never met the person, but you can tell from her tone of voice and the words she uses to describe them that she doesn't like the person at all or that she likes the person a lot. That's **CONTEXT**: the things around something that help us understand it.

EXAMPLE:

Say you see a man with a big hose. Why does he have it? What kind of person is he? That depends on the context!

If he's filling a swimming pool, he might be the caretaker of a pool.

If he's shooting it at a burning building, he might be a fireman.

If he's watering a plant, he might be a master gardener.

USING CONTEXT to DEFINE a WORD

The same thing goes for words—sometimes we don't know what a word means, but we can still figure out something about it from context in the sentence.

EXAMPLE:

Some people like lions, and others like tigers, but I prefer bandersnatches.

From the comparison to people who like lions or tigers, you can guess that a bandersnatch is probably:

1. an animal like a lion or tiger
2. somehow different from a lion or tiger
3. perhaps better than a lion or tiger

"BANDERSNATCH" is an imaginary word created by Lewis Carroll.

68

We can use context to guess the meaning of words in nonfiction, too. Like in this passage from THE AUTOBIOGRAPHY OF BENJAMIN FRANKLIN:

There was a salt-marsh that bounded part of the mill-pond, on the edge of which, at high water, we used to stand to fish for minnows. By much trampling, we had made it a mere quagmire. My proposal was to build a wharff there fit for us to stand upon, and I showed my comrades a large heap of stones, which were intended for a new house near the marsh, and which would very well suit our purpose. Accordingly, in the evening, when the workmen were gone, I assembled a number of my play-fellows, and working with them diligently like so many emmets, sometimes two or three to a stone, we brought them all away and built our little wharff. The next morning the workmen were surprised at missing the stones, which were found in our wharff. Inquiry was made after the removers; we were discovered and complained of; several of us were corrected by our fathers; and though I pleaded the usefulness of the work, mine convinced me that nothing was useful which was not honest.

EXAMPLE:

What in the world is a "quagmire"?

First, look at what else is around it.
* It's on the edge of a marsh, so it's probably wet or damp.
* It happens when you trample down the edge of a marsh.
* It's not as nice as a marsh, because he calls it "a mere quagmire," as if it's worse than it was before.

Second, take an educated guess. I would guess a "quagmire" is something watery and not very pleasant. If we look up "quagmire" in a dictionary, it describes land that is so soaked with water that it's not solid anymore . . . pretty close to the definition we arrived at just by context!

EXAMPLE:

What's an "emmet"?

First, look at what else is around it.

* * "A number" and "so many" makes me think there are lots of them.
* * "Working diligently" means good workers.
* * "Sometimes two or three to a stone," so his friends are working together.

Then, take an educated guess. I would guess an "emmet" is an animal that often works hard with many other emmets—possibly to build things. If we look up "emmet" in a dictionary, it turns out it is an old word for ants—who do work hard, work together, and build things!

STOP CALLING ME "EMMET"! YOU SOUND SO OLD-FASHIONED!

1. Define "context."

2. Someone asks you, "What does 'expository' mean?" Are there any context clues in the question that help you answer the person?

3. True or false: You can use context clues to figure out the meaning of words but not phrases.

4. Based on the context in the following sentence, was the bandersnatch red?

   The bandersnatch was the same color as the cloudless sky.

5. Based on the context of the following sentence, does it make sense to be afraid of bandersnatches?

   They were harmless as lambs, but Mrs. Withers still had an unreasonable fear of bandersnatches.

6. True or false: You can use context clues to better understand unfamiliar words in both fiction and nonfiction.

7. Based on the context of the following sentence, what physical characteristic do all bandersnatches share?

I thought this bandersnatch was going to be different, but it's got four wings and a love of chewing gum like all the rest of them.

8. Based on the context of the following sentence, what do all bandersnatches have in common?

Some prefer newspapers and some like novels, but I've never met a bandersnatch who didn't have something to read with them.

9. What does context help us understand?

10. Based on the context of the following sentence, does "frumious" describe a taste or a smell?

The bandersnatch was so frumious that the whole place smelled like pickles.

ANSWERS

CHECK YOUR ANSWERS

1. The words around an unknown word that help you define it or understand it better

2. No

3. False

4. No

5. No

6. True

7. Four wings and a love of chewing gum

8. They like to read.

9. The meaning of unknown words.

10. A smell

Chapter 8

LATIN and GREEK AFFIXES and ROOTS

AFFIXES and ROOTS

Some word parts show up again and again in different words.

EXAMPLES:

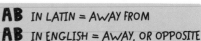

AB IN LATIN = AWAY FROM
AB IN ENGLISH = AWAY, OR OPPOSITE

ABsurd: not reasonable (or away from what is reasonable)

ABnormal: not normal (or away from what is normal)

ABsolutely: without restriction (or away from restrictions)

MILe: 5,280 feet or 1,760 yards

MILlennium: a thousand years

MILlion: a thousand thousands!

1,000 × 1,000 = 1 MILLION

That's because the English language is made up of many other languages. Sometimes parts of those other languages show up in English. They can show up in two different places: as the **ROOT** of a word, or as an **AFFIX**.

> **ROOT**
> the most basic part of a word
> without any affixes

Roots

Roots are the most basic part of a word. A root word often holds the core of the word's meaning.

ROOT

EXAMPLES:

USE: employ something to get a result

USEful: able to be used

misUSE: used incorrectly

The root "use" means employ something to get a result. When we add affixes, like "full" or "mis," we change the meaning of the root word and form a new word.

Affixes

Affixes have different names, depending on where they appear in a word. If they appear at the front of a root word, they're called **PREFIXES**.

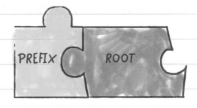

EXAMPLES:

COMpromise: to make an agreement with someone

COMpanion: someone who is with another person

COM = WITH

INTERnational: between nations

INTERstate: between states

INTER = BETWEEN

If an affix shows up at the end of a word, it's called a **SUFFIX**.

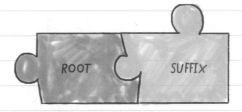

EXAMPLES:

EdIBLE: capable of being eaten

PresentABLE: capable of being presented

ABLE/IBLE = CAPABLE OF BEING

BlameLESS: without blame

endLESS: without end

LESS = WITHOUT

77

LATIN and GREEK

Prefixes and suffixes may seem like some crazy code. In a way, they are—they're in a "code" based on the original Latin and Greek. But once we learn the meanings of common roots and affixes, we can "crack the code." Even when we don't know a word, we can make good guesses about what it might mean, based on the part we recognize from other words.

> You can even see how roots and affixes work with the names of these word parts themselves:
>
> **AF** = IN ADDITION TO, LIKE IN "AFTER" → **AFFIX**
>
> **PREFIX** ← **PRE** = BEFORE, LIKE IN "PREVIEW"
>
> **SUFFIX** ← **SUF** = BELOW, LIKE IN "SUFFER"
>
> *Fix* is the root. It appears in all three words, and it means "to be attached to something else."

You don't have to know all of Latin and Greek to break the code. Just knowing the most common Latin and Greek roots and affixes will help you understand thousands of words, like these:

KNOWING ROOTS AND AFFIXES HELPS US FIGURE OUT WORDS IN ALL SUBJECTS—ESPECIALLY SCIENCE AND MATH CLASS!

ROOT/ AFFIX	LANGUAGE	TRANSLATION	EXAMPLE
ANTI	Greek	Against	Antifreeze
ASTRO	Greek	Star	Astronaut
BENE	Latin	Good	Benefit
BI	Greek	Two	Bisect
CHRON	Greek	Time	Chronology
COSM	Greek	World	Cosmos
CRACY	Greek	Government	Democracy
CYCL	Greek	Circle, Wheel	Bicycle
DEM	Greek	People	Democracy
DICT	Latin	Say	Dictate
GEO*	Greek	Earth	Geology
GEN	Latin	Birth	Genesis
MECH	Greek	Machine	Mechanic

You can figure out the whole word "bicycle" from knowing "bi" and "cycl."

79

ROOT/ AFFIX	LANGUAGE	TRANSLATION	EXAMPLE
MIS	Latin	Send	Missile
OLOGY	Greek	Study	Geology
PHON	Greek	Sound	Telephone
PORT	Latin	Carry	Portable
PYRO	Greek	Fire	Pyrotechnics
SCOPE	Greek	See	Telescope
TERR *	Latin	Earth	Terrestrial
VIS	Latin	See	Visible

* GEO and TERR: These roots mean the same thing in different languages!

1. Would a suffix go at the beginning of a word?

2. What do you take away from a word to find its root?

3. What ancient language, along with Greek, forms many roots and affixes in English?

4. Based on the following words, what do you think the root "aud" might mean?

   Audible, auditorium, audience

5. If "scope" means to see, would you expect a spectroscope to measure light or to measure sound?

6. Can an affix appear at the end of a word?

7. If a word contained both a prefix and a suffix, which would come first?

8. "Geocycle" isn't a word. But if it was, what two meanings might it contain?

9. Think of one other word that contains the root "cycle."

10. How does the word you chose relate to a wheel or circle?

ANSWERS

CHECK YOUR ANSWERS

1. No

2. All affixes

3. Latin

4. To hear

5. Light

6. Yes

7. Prefix

8. The earth and a wheel

9. Bicycle, tricycle, recycle, unicycle, cyclist, motorcycle, cyclone, encyclopedia

10. A tricycle has three wheels.

#9 and #10 have more than one correct answer.

Chapter 9

REFERENCE MATERIALS

REFERENCE MATERIALS

Have you got a question about something? REFERENCE MATERIALS are where you go to look things up or find out more about something. There are different kinds of reference materials to consult, based on the kind of question you have.

GLOSSARY

THESAURUS
DICTIONARY

What Does It Mean?

You're reading along and you come to a word you don't know. What does it mean? That's when you reach for a **DICTIONARY**. A dictionary is a reference book or an online resource that lists words in alphabetical order, with entries about what the words mean and how to pronounce them.

The entry about a word's meaning is called a **DEFINITION**.
A good definition tells you <u>five things</u>:

1. the word being defined
2. the part of speech
3. the syllables
4. the pronunciation
5. what that word means

EXAMPLE:

THIS IS THE WORD
BEING DEFINED.   THE PART OF SPEECH

Immense *adjective* im·mense \i-'men(t)s\   THIS IS THE PHONETIC
SPELLING—THIS GIVES US
THE PRONUNCIATION.

THIS TELLS US
THE NUMBER OF
SYLLABLES.

By permission. From *Merriam-Webster's Collegiate® Dictionary, 11ᵗʰ Edition*
©2016 by Merriam-Webster, Inc. (www.Merriam-Webster.com).

A word doesn't only mean just one
thing. A definition will also tell us
all the possible things a word can
mean, some other forms of the
word, and examples of how the word is used.

> **PRONUNCIATION**
> how to say something aloud

EXAMPLE:

Immense *adjective* im·mense \i-'men(t)s\

1: marked by greatness especially in size or degree; *especially*: transcending ordinary means of measurement <the *immense* universe>

2: supremely good
—im·mense·ly *adverb*
—im·mense·ness *noun*

Examples of IMMENSE
  He inherited an *immense* fortune.
  She is an artist of *immense* talent.

A **GLOSSARY** is like a dictionary, but it only has some words relating to a specific topic. For example, say you were reading a book about sailing. You might understand all the words except the ones that have to do with sailing, like **STARBOARD, PORT, LEE, GALLEY**, and **BRIG**. That's where a glossary comes in handy. It'll tell you the meanings of words that are specific to a special situation. There's a good chance you'll find one at the back of the book you're reading.

What's a starboard? Is it like a surfboard covered in stars?

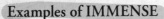

brig: *noun* \\'brig\\
a 2-masted square-rigged ship

galley: *noun* gal·ley \\'gəl-ē\\
1: a large low ship of olden times moved by oars and sails
2: the kitchen especially of a ship or airplane

lee: *noun* \\'lē\\
1: protecting shelter
2: the side (as of a ship) or area that is sheltered from the wind

port: *noun* \\'pȯrt\\
1: a place where ships may ride secure from storms: haven
2: a harbor town or city where ships may take on or discharge cargo

starboard: *noun* star·board \\'stär-bərd\\
the side of a ship or aircraft that is on the right when you are
looking toward the front

What's Another Word for . . . ?

There are a lot of words in the world, but sometimes we use the same ones over and over. What if we get tired of the same old words? What if we want to find just the right word to say what we mean? That's when we reach for a **THESAURUS**.

A rare kind of dinosaur

thesaurus

Say you want to say something is beautiful, but you don't want to use the word "beautiful" or you want to communicate a kind of beauty. Just flip open your thesaurus to the "beautiful" entry, or go online and look up "beautiful" on a credible thesaurus site. It might contain words like:

THESAURUS
a book that groups words with other words that mean similar things

Alluring, cute, dazzling, exquisite, good-looking, gorgeous, ideal, lovely, magnificent, pretty, splendid, sublime, superb, wonderful

MANY OF THESE WORDS SUIT ME PERFECTLY!

Now you've got options! You can add some variety to what you say or write.

You can also write more clearly, because no two words mean exactly the same thing. So now you can choose just the right one—but be careful! The word "beautiful" might mean all of these things, but not all of these things mean the SAME thing. You probably wouldn't call a daisy "good-looking," for instance. Or say that an icy glacier was "cute."

WHO YOU CALLING "GOOD-LOOKING"?

A thesaurus doesn't give you a set of interchangeable words, but it does give you a lot of great options to choose from.

How Do I Pronounce It?

Once we know what a word means, we want to use it. If we look something up in the dictionary, we can see how it's spelled. But how do we **SAY** it? The PRONUNCIATION GUIDE is the part of the definition that tells us how to pronounce the word.

IS THIS EVEN ENGLISH?

EXAMPLE:

Immense *adjective* im·mense \i-'men(t)s\

It may look like it's in a foreign language, but those strange characters tell us how to pronounce the word.

First of all, it tells us there are two syllables separated by a hypen (-). In phonetic rendering, the small "i" stands for the short "i" sound. That's how we know it uses the same sound as "impossible" instead of the long "i" in "like" or "line." The fact that the "t" is shown in parentheses tells us that we don't really say it aloud. It's silent! Which is why it's hidden there between the parentheses.

Most dictionaries include a guide to pronunciation symbols. Also, a lot of online dictionaries have a "read aloud" function, so you can hear the word being spoken aloud.

PRONUNCIATION KEY: QUICK REFERENCE

\ə\ as **a** in abut

\'ə ˌə\ as **u** in abut

\ə\ as **e** in kitten

\ə r\ as **ur/er** in further

\a\ as **a** in ash

\ā\ as **a** in ace

\ä\ as **o** in mop

\aů\ as **ou** in out

\b\ as **b** in baby

\ch\ as **ch** in chin

\d\ as **d** in did

\e\ as **e** in bet

\'ē ˌē\ as **ea** in easy

\ē\ as **y** in easy

\f\ as **f** in fifty

\g\ as **g** in go

\h\ as **h** in hat

\i\ as **i** in hit

\ī\ as **i** in ice

\j\ as **j** in job

\k\ as **k** in kin

\k̲\ as **ch** in ich dien

\l\ as **l** in lily

\m\ as **m** in murmur

\n\ as **n** in own

\ŋ\ as **ng** in sing

\ō\ as **o** in go

\ȯ\ as **aw** in law

\ȯ i\ as **oy** in boy

\p\ as **p** in pepper

\r\ as **r** in red

\s\ as **s** in less

\sh\ as **sh** in shy

\t\ as **t** in tie

\th\ as **th** in thin

\th̲\ as **th** in the

\ü\ as **oo** in loot

\ů\ as **oo** in foot

\v\ as **v** in vivid

\w\ as **w** in away

\y\ as **y** in yet

\yü\ as **you** in youth

\yů\ as **u** in curable

\z\ as **z** in zone

\zh\ as **si** in vision

By permission. From *Merriam-Webster's Collegiate Dictionary, 11th Edition*
©2016 by Merriam-Webster, Inc. (www.Merriam-Webster.com).

CHECK YOUR KNOWLEDGE

1. What is a dictionary full of?

2. What do you call a smaller dictionary full of words that are used only in specific situations?

3. Would you find an entry like this in a dictionary or a thesaurus?

   Ugly, grotesque, hideous, unsightly

4. Does a word's part of speech belong in a dictionary entry?

5. If you wanted to find just the right word to describe a specific situation, would you use a glossary or a thesaurus?

6. If you were trying to understand the vocabulary a lawyer uses in a contract, would you use a glossary or a thesaurus?

7. What part of a definition would you look at if you wanted to know how to say a word aloud?

8. Will a dictionary definition ever tell you more than one meaning for a word?

9. Which contains most of the words in an entire language, a dictionary or glossary?

10. If you want to find a word to tell your friend how much you care about her but you don't want to use the word "care," would you use a dictionary, thesaurus, or glossary?

CHECK YOUR ANSWERS

1. Words and their definitions, as well as pronunciations and examples

2. Glossary

3. Thesaurus

4. Yes

5. Thesaurus

6. Glossary

7. The pronunciation guide

8. Yes

9. Dictionary

10. Thesaurus

unit 2

LANGUAGE

Language isn't just a bunch of words in a dictionary or rules in a grammar book. It's the whole **WAY** we talk and write, including the way we play with words, the ways words work together to form whole new meanings, and all the little choices we make along the way to say just what we want to say.

Chapter 10

FIGURATIVE LANGUAGE

FIGURES of SPEECH

A **FIGURE OF SPEECH** is language that isn't **LITERAL**, straightforward, or factual. A figure of speech is the opposite of LITERAL LANGUAGE, which states the facts, and nothing but the facts.

> **LITERAL**
> an understanding of words at their most basic sense

EXAMPLE:

Instead of writing, "It's raining hard out there," we might write, "It's raining cats and dogs." We don't mean that puppies and kittens are literally falling from the sky.

So why would we write it that way? Well, it's more interesting, and figures of speech can amplify what we're trying to communicate. People will pay more attention to what we're saying . . . and be more likely to remember it. That's called RHETORICAL FORCE: the way we use words to make our points clear, interesting, and memorable.

But it's important to be able to recognize the difference between figurative and literal language, otherwise we might think cats and dogs are *literally* falling from the sky.

Personification

PERSONIFICATION is a figure of speech that pretends that something that isn't human has human qualities.

EXAMPLES:

The sky was weeping.

When the sun came up, the roses lifted their faces.

Luc's belly growled.

GRRR...

Allusion

ALLUSION is when we refer to something without

LIKE AN
INSIDE
JOKE

mentioning it directly. We use allusions when we want to remind someone of something but not mention it directly.

Allusions DON'T work when the reader doesn't get what we're writing about. So in general, we make allusions to things that the reader knows about, too. Often the stories that the reader knows are the stories that MANY people know.

BIBLICAL ALLUSION

BIBLICAL ALLUSIONS are allusions that refer to stories that originally came from the Bible.

EXAMPLE:

"I'm going into the lion's den."

Someone might say this on the way into a meeting. They don't really mean that the meeting will be full of lions. They're really saying that they're going into a tough situation by referring to a story from the Bible—the story of Daniel, who was put into a den of lions by an angry king.

LITERARY ALLUSION

LITERARY ALLUSIONS are allusions that refer to a story in literature.

EXAMPLE:

He's an old Scrooge.

The writer isn't saying the person's name is Scrooge or even that he is old. The writer is probably saying this person doesn't like to spend money by making a LITERARY ALLUSION to Charles Dickens's famous story A CHRISTMAS CAROL. In A CHRISTMAS CAROL, a character named Scrooge loves his money so much that he hates to spend it on anything or anyone.

MYTHOLOGICAL ALLUSION

MYTHOLOGICAL ALLUSIONS are allusions that refer to stories from **MYTHOLOGY**.

> **MYTHOLOGY**
> a collection of myths, often from a specific culture or religion

EXAMPLE:

While Kate is a talented player, her quick temper is her Achilles' heel.

The phrase "Achilles' heel" is a mythological allusion to the character Achilles from Greek mythology. His only vulnerable spot was the back of his heel—he could not be harmed otherwise. However, even that small weakness proved to be a fatal flaw; he later died by being struck in his heel with an arrow. The sentence above is explaining that the girl's quick temper is her only flaw, but it has big consequences.

UH-OH.

Verbal Irony

IRONY is when we say the <u>opposite</u> of what we mean. Why would we do that? It makes the material more interesting and can actually emphasize what we really mean to say.

EXAMPLE:

If someone asks if you'd like to go outside, but it's raining, you might say:

"Of course I would! There's nothing I'd like more than getting soaked in the rain."

When you use verbal irony here, you aren't just saying no. You're explaining why you wouldn't like to go outside by contrasting that with the opposite idea. The difference between the two thoughts expresses what you really mean.

Puns

A **PUN** is a joke that uses the different meanings of a word or a play on words that sound alike. William Shakespeare was a master at writing puns, like this one from ROMEO AND JULIET. Here, two friends—Mercutio and Romeo—are talking about dancing:

EXAMPLE:

MERCUTIO: "Nay, gentle Romeo, we must have you dance."

ROMEO: "Not I, believe me. You have dancing shoes / With nimble soles; I have a soul of lead. . . ."

How does this pun work? It "puns" because the words "soul" and "sole" sound the same but have different meanings (and different spellings). Shakespeare is using a pun to emphasize the difference between Mercutio, who wants to dance and celebrate, and Romeo, who is heartbroken and wants to be left alone. The pun tells us a lot about Mercutio and Romeo—one focuses on his physical feelings while the other focuses on his emotional feelings.

1. Does a pun make a reference to a biblical story?

2. If you wanted to say something that was literally true, would you use a figure of speech?

3. What do mythological allusions refer to?

4. What type of figure of speech is in the following sentence: "Our old house groaned and whined during the hurricane."

5. If an allusion refers to something that happened in a novel, what kind of allusion is it?

6. What kind of figure of speech says the opposite of what it means?

7. What kind of figure of speech makes a joke based on the fact that words have more than one meaning?

8. If an allusion refers to a story from the Bible, what kind of allusion is it?

9. Does verbal irony depend on words that sound alike?

10. What kind of allusion does the following sentence make?
"I think the god of thunder lives in the apartment above us."

CHECK YOUR ANSWERS

1. No

2. No

3. Myths and mythical characters

4. Personification

5. Literary

6. Verbal irony

7. Pun

8. Biblical

9. No

10. Mythological

Chapter 11

WORD RELATIONSHIPS

WORD RELATIONSHIPS and MEANINGS

Words don't just exist in a vacuum out in space. Sometimes we can only **REALLY** understand what they mean because of the words around them.

EXAMPLES:

"I love strawberries!"

"I love my mom!"

"Love" is the same word in both places. Its definition doesn't change, but we probably don't feel the same feelings toward strawberries and our moms. We can only know what "love" means in this sentence by looking at the words around it—that's what a WORD RELATIONSHIP is!

Cause/Effect Word Relationships

Sometimes you can tell what a word means by the **EFFECT** it has **CAUSED** on another word.

> **CAUSE**
> source of a change
> or effect

COMMON CAUSE AND EFFECT WORDS

> **EFFECT**
> result or outcome

"SO" EXAMPLE:

CAUSE →

EFFECT ↓

[We ran out of sugar] before we finished baking, [so we had to go to the store.]

"BECAUSE" EXAMPLE:

EFFECT — CAUSE

[I wanted a new bike,] [because I saw the one that Carlos had.]

CAUSE COMES BEFORE EFFECT IN LIFE . . . BUT NOT ALWAYS IN A SENTENCE!

"SINCE" EXAMPLE:

CAUSE — EFFECT

[Since I learned scales,] [I can hear a song's key more easily.]

Items and Categories

Sometimes you learn more about a word because it's part of a **CATEGORY**.

CATEGORY
a group of things or people that share qualities

FOR INSTANCE: There are 18 students in the class.

ITEM — CATEGORY

We can learn about both STUDENTS and CLASSES because they are related as items in a category.

What do we learn about students?

 They are part of a class!

What do we learn about classes?

 They are made up of students!

Synonyms and Antonyms

Imagine you're about to introduce your brother to a new friend. You want to give your brother an idea of what the new

COMPARE
find the
similarities

friend will be like when he arrives. You might say, "He's just like Chris." Or you might

CONTRAST
find the
differences

say, "He's nothing like Chris." Either way, if your brother knows Chris, he'll understand something about your new friend when you **COMPARE** or **CONTRAST** the two of them.

The same is true with words. If you know that a word is like another word, then you know something about its meaning.

SYNONYM
word with the
same meaning

If you know it's different from another word, you know something about it, too. Words that mean the same thing are called **SYNONYMS**. Words that mean the opposite of each other are called **ANTONYMS**.

ANTONYM
word with the
opposite meaing

EXAMPLES:

ORIGINAL WORD	SYNONYM	ANTONYM
♡ love	👍 like, care	hate, dislike ✗
good	fine	bad
safe	secure	dangerous
give	share	take
healthy	well	sick
new	recent	old
soft	gentle	hard
victory	triumph ♕	defeat ☠

Analogy

An **ANALOGY** compares two things that are similar in some important way.

EXAMPLES:

A student is to a new topic like a detective is to a case.

My brother is to me like my uncle is to my mom.

A:B::X:Y RELATIONSHIPS

Many analogies come in the form
"A is to B like X is to Y" or A:B::X:Y.

Analogies can show different relationships, like synonyms, antonyms, a part to a whole, cause and effect, and more.

EXAMPLES:

Medicine : sickness :: water : thirst

Wing : bird :: fin : whale

Albany : New York :: Springfield : Illinois

Paltry : trivial :: considerable : important

However, an extended analogy draws the comparison out and may make other comparisons based on the first one.

Like this one from Shakespeare's comedy AS YOU LIKE IT:

1st analogy: If the world is a stage...

All the world's a stage,   ...then everybody in the world must be an actor.

And all the men and women merely players;

on and off stage/in and out of life

They have their exits and their entrances,

And one man in his time plays many parts,

His acts being seven ages.   We play different roles—like student, friend, sibling, etc.

We do the things that actors do: play parts, have exits (die) and entrances (are born), do acts.

PART AND WHOLE WORD RELATIONSHIPS

Sometimes words are related because one object is part of a whole object. Some analogies compare a part to its whole.

EXAMPLES:

A piece is to pie like a slice is to pizza.

A runner is to a relay race team like a musician is to a band.

We may understand unfamiliar words or relationships better when we read a comparison. We can also explain complex concepts clearly by writing them as comparisons. However, the comparisons have to work, or the analogies won't make sense.

EXAMPLE:

A tree is to a forest like a boat is to an ocean.

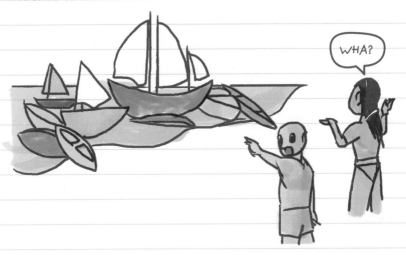

This analogy just doesn't work. Forests are made out of trees, but the ocean isn't made out of boats. To fix it, write about what the ocean is really full of . . . water!

A tree is to a forest like a drop of water is to an ocean.

CHECK YOUR KNOWLEDGE

1. Is the word "since" used to describe cause and effect or something that is part of a whole?

2. Fill in the blank:
   An astronaut steers her rocket like a bus driver steers his ___.

3. Is "hate" a synonym for "love"?

4. Define "antonym."

5. What is the cause in this sentence?
   I went running because I needed some exercise.

6. True or false: An analogy compares two or more sets of things that have nothing in common.

7. Is "sad" an antonym for "happy"?

8. Fill in the blank:
   Petal : flower :: feather : ____

9. Is "so" a word you could use in a sentence describing cause and effect?

10. What two things are being compared in this analogy?
The sun appeared on the horizon as if someone had just carried a lantern over the crest of a hill.

ANSWERS ➤ 117

CHECK YOUR ANSWERS

1. Cause and effect

2. Bus

3. No

4. An antonym is a word with the opposite meaning.

5. I needed some exercise.

6. False

7. Yes

8. Bird

9. Yes

10. The sun and a lantern

Chapter 12

NUANCES in WORD MEANINGS

NUANCE

NUANCE is a subtle difference in meaning.

> **"NUANCE"**
> comes from the French word for "shade"—as in, shades of meaning.

EXAMPLE:

"Sweetie, come here . . ."

VS.

"Alex Christopher Johnson, get over here!"

The words in each sentence mean the same basic thing:

> Sweetie = Alex Christopher Johnson
> come here = get over here

But they have different traces of significance and **INTENTION**.

By having a strong understanding of a word's nuance, you can communicate effectively by using the words with just the right meanings. You can use a word's

nuance to emphasize different features of what you are describing. For example, "not good" means basically the same thing as "bad." "Bad" is roughly the same as "terrible." Lastly, "terrible" is close in meaning to "disastrous." However, if your friend asks, "How was your day?" there's a big difference between saying "Not good" and "Disastrous!"

Why are those two answers so different? A word's **DENOTATION** and **CONNOTATION** can greatly impact the idea being communicated.

DENOTION
the dictionary definition of a word

A word is usually used according to its connotation because of the way that word can change the meaning of a sentence.

CONNOTATION
an idea or feeling that a word communicates, which can subtly color the word's meaning

120

EXAMPLE:

In this paragraph from Alexandre Dumas's THE COUNT OF MONTE CRISTO, the author describes Danglars, the enemy of Edmond Dantes (the hero). What if we switched the underlined words with similar words?

He was a man of twenty-five or twenty-six years of age, of unprepossessing countenance, obsequious to his superiors, insolent to his subordinates; and this, in addition to his position as responsible agent on board, which is always obnoxious to the sailors, made him as much disliked by the crew as Edmond Dantes was beloved by them.

MONTE CRISTO

WORD	SYNONYMS FROM A THESAURUS
Unprepossessing	Unattractive, awful, disfigured, grotesque, etc.
Obsequious	Respectful, servile, obedient, fawning, slavish, etc.
Insolent	Arrogant, breezy, discourteous, etc.

For "UNPREPOSSESSING," all of the synonyms mean "unpleasant to look at." But the connotations are different. "Unattractive" is hardly the same thing as "disfigured."

For "OBSEQUIOUS," all of the synonyms mean "showing regard for power." But the connotations are not alike. "Fawning" can mean that you make a fool of yourself trying to get someone to like you. Meanwhile, "respectful" has the connotation that you keep your own dignity as you show respect to another person.

For "INSOLENT," the denotations of the synonyms are similar: showing a lack of respect. But their connotations may clash with the original idea. "Arrogant" signifies that you think a lot of yourself. "Breezy" expresses that you take things lightly, which could be good or bad, depending on the situation. "Discourteous" means you're rude. "Insulting" means you are discrediting someone or something else.

In fact, if we replace the original words with synonyms that have similar meanings, without thinking about nuance, the passage might communicate something totally different, like this:

He was a man of twenty-five or twenty-six years of age, of grotesque countenance, respectful to his superiors, breezy to his subordinates; and this, in addition to his position as responsible agent on board, which is always obnoxious to the sailors, made him as much disliked by the crew as Edmond Dantes was beloved by them.

All these words have similar denotations as the original words, but the connotations aren't the same. In the original description, Danglars sounds like a real villain. But in this version, he doesn't sound like such a bad guy, although the passage doesn't make much sense anymore. In fact, from the changed description, it's hard to tell why the sailors WOULDN'T like him. That's the power of nuance!

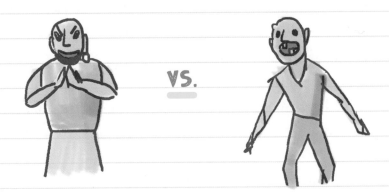

VS.

1. "Nuance" comes from a French word that means what?

2. A nuance is a subtle difference in _____.

3. You replace a word in a sentence and it has the same meaning but a different nuance than the replaced word. Can the meaning of the sentence change just because the nuance of the word changed?

4. Does "denotation" mean the way a word gets used in everyday life?

5. Is "denotation" the same thing as a "definition"?

6. Do "jealous" and "doubting" have the same denotation of feeling envy?

7. Do "yard" and "lawn" have the same denotation of a small area of grass?

8. Do "president" and "king" have the same connotations?

9. Do "czar," "king," and "raja" all have the denotation of "ruler"?

10. Do "house" and "mansion" have the same denotation?

CHECK YOUR ANSWERS

1. Shade   **2.** Meaning   **3.** Yes

4. No   **5.** Yes

6. No—"jealous" does denote feeling envy, but "doubtful" denotes feeling uncertain.

7. Yes, both mean a small area of grass. You can contrast them with similar words, like "field," "pasture," and "meadow," that denote a larger area of grass.

8. No, because a president is usually an appointed figure in government, while a king is usually someone who inherits his position.

9. Yes, because "ruler" is a large enough category to describe all three: czar, king, and raja.

10. No

Unit 3
READING FICTION

Fiction is writing that isn't drawn from real life—all of the scenes, characters, and stories come from a person's imagination. There are all kinds of ways to tell an imaginative story: not just books and short stories, but plays and poetry, too. Reading fiction means understanding all the elements that make up a story, like plot, character, dialogue, and tone—even the author's own life stories and how those experiences affect what he or she writes. All of it comes together to make reading fiction great.

A fictional story always comes from a person's imagination, but that's not to say that fiction can't be realistic—a fictional piece of writing can be based on a reality that exists and/or it can be based on something that is completely impossible.

Chapter 13

TYPES OF FICTION

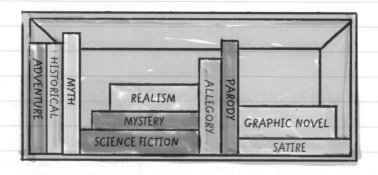

FICTION GENRES

GENRE is just a fancy name for what *kind* of literature you're reading. Take "adventure," for instance. If you pick up an adventure story, you don't expect to read a book that's mostly about two people falling in love. Or a poem about a moral lesson. No, you expect action.

I ♥ ACTION

The kinds of action might vary, but no matter how different one adventure story may be from another, you still expect some danger and thrills. There are many different fiction genres, and each has its own characteristics.

"GENRE" comes from the French word *genre*, which means "kind," as in type, sort, or style.

STORIES

Stories, well . . . they tell a story! They can be short stories, novels, or even told live by a person who's right in front of you. But all fiction stories have one thing in common: They describe imaginary events to entertain us or to teach us—or both!

Common Story Genres

ADVENTURE: full of thrills and action

HISTORICAL FICTION: based on historical events, but not necessarily historical facts

ROMANCE: about love

MYSTERY: centered on solving a puzzle, strange problem, or crime

MYTH: cultural story usually involving supernatural characters

SCIENCE FICTION: based on the possibilities of future science or technology

FANTASY: fiction that has elements of magic and other supernatural phenomena at the center of the story

PARODY: a story that imitates another piece of art to make fun of the work; a spoof

KEEP CALM AND STUDY ON

SATIRE: a story that uses humor to expose stupidity or corruption in the world

GRAPHIC NOVEL: a novel told in sequential art, like a comic strip

ALLEGORY: a story that contains a hidden meaning

REALISM: fiction stories that try to depict real, everyday life

Just like people, stories don't always fit neatly into categories. A lot of stories connect to more than one genre—a piece of fiction can include features from more than one genre or blend genres to create something unique.

DRAMA

A **DRAMA** is a special kind of story. Dramas are texts of plays that are recited by actors—usually in costume and surrounded by sets onstage, in film, or on television.

> **"DRAMA"**
> comes from the Greek and Latin word *drama:* "to do or act."

Common Drama Genres

* **ONE-ACT PLAY:** only contains a single **ACT**

* **MULTI-ACT PLAY:** contains more than one act

> **ACT**
> a main division in a play, like a chapter in a book

* **SCREENPLAYS:** dramas intended to be made into films or television

Act 1

Act 2

POETRY

POETRY doesn't have any single definition. But if you see a piece of literature with an unusual style, formatting, special rhythm, or rhymes, and if it's about thoughts or intense feelings, there's a good chance it's poetry.

Common Poetry Genres

* **FREE VERSE**: poems that have no set rhyme or **METER**

  There are many young adult novels that are written in free verse now, too.

METER
the rhythm of a poem

* **LYRIC**: songlike poems that usually focus on emotions

* **EPIC**: long poems about serious events, usually focused on a hero

There are many types of poems, such as sonnets, odes, ballads, and more!

WHAT'S the DIFFERENCE?

Depending on the genre, the same story can sound very different. For instance, imagine you're telling a story about a young woman who leaves her sweetheart behind to travel around the world in search of a magic key that will restore the fortunes of her father, the king. Depending on what you want to emphasize, you might choose very different genres to work in. And depending on what structure you choose, what you write may even have different meanings.

EXAMPLES:

Genre:
ADVENTURE STORY

Agatha paused in the doorway, listening. A set of footsteps approached down the long, dark hall. Even though she couldn't see anything, her fingers tightened around the dagger in her belt. . . .

Notes:
→ Concentrates on the thrilling details and creating suspense
→ Fast-paced storytelling
→ Not much reflection or description

Genre:
MYSTERY STORY

Agatha rifled through the drawers as quickly as she could. She found old gum wrappers, a letter opener, a pair of eyeglasses, and several packs of unopened mint gum—but nothing that shed any light on her only question: Where in the world did the magic key go?

Notes:
→ Concentrates on the unsolved elements
→ More about what's happening in her mind than in the rest of the world

Genre:
MULTI-ACT PLAY

NOT IF YOU NEVER CATCH ME!

POLICE INSPECTOR: There you are! You'll never get away with this!

AGATHA: *(Jumps through window to ground below, and calls over her shoulder as she runs away)* Not if you never catch me!

Notes:
→ Written for actors; not much opportunity to show characters' thoughts, unless they say them aloud or perform them through movement
→ Includes stage directions, props, and other theater elements

Genre:
LYRIC POETRY

Beautiful Agatha,
Her lonely suitor dreamed,
If I just love her long enough
Then she'll come home to me.

Notes:
→ Doesn't say much about action
→ Concentrates on feelings
→ Has rhymes like a song

Genre:
EPIC POEM

Agatha crossed oceans
Under sun and moon
And after all her labors
She brought the old key home.

Notes:
→ Doesn't say much about feelings and thoughts
→ Concentrates on the big picture and action
→ Focuses on Agatha as a hero

Different genres alter the focus or meaning of a piece of literature, so authors usually choose their genres carefully and for a purpose. An author who wants to focus on a love story, for instance, probably wouldn't write an epic, because he would have to include so much adventure that doesn't have much to do with the love story. On the other hand, an author who was more interested in playing with language than telling a story might choose a lyric poem, where the way something is expressed is the focus of the genre.

WHAT'S THE EXPERIENCE?

Even the very same piece of literature can become different depending on how we experience it. These are various ways to experience literature:

AUDIO:

* We don't read the words, we just listen to someone reading them to us.

* We use our imagination to "see" what's happening.

EXAMPLES: audiobooks, being read to by a parent, radio programs, podcasts, etc.

VISUAL:

* We <u>see</u> most of what is being written about.

* Instead of using our imagination to visualize the text, we have to connect the images we see with whatever is given.

* We don't get to imagine visual details for ourselves.

EXAMPLES: comic books, graphic novels, picture books, etc.

LIVE:

* There's a person—or people—right in front of us <u>performing</u> the text!

* We can't put the book down in the middle of the story—we have to watch until it's done!

EXAMPLES: plays, **MONOLOGUES**, poetry slams, etc.

MONOLOGUE
a long speech by one
actor in a play

MULTIMEDIA:

* A <u>combination</u> of different ways of experiencing the text. Instead of just hearing or seeing, we see and hear—and sometimes even feel—the text!

EXAMPLES: animation, TV, musicals, simulators, interactive websites, virtual reality, etc.

CHECK YOUR KNOWLEDGE

1. Does a writer of historical fiction ever change the true facts of history?

2. Is adventure the genre that focuses on solving a mystery?

3. Can a play contain more than one act?

4. If you hear a story read while images are being projected on a screen, are you having a multimedia experience?

5. Can the meaning of a story change depending on whether it is written as an epic poem or a lyric poem?

6. What kind of poem tells a serious story, usually involving a hero?

7. What genre makes fun of the style of another artist?

8. A story about a boy who is turned into a lion is an example of what genre or genres?

9. A story about two friends who have crushes on each other but can't get up the nerve to tell each other is an example of what genre or genres?

10. A poem about two sisters who sail across the world to solve the mystery of their missing brother is an example of what genre or genres?

CHECK YOUR ANSWERS

1. Yes

2. No

3. Yes

4. Yes

5. Yes

6. Epic

7. Parody

8. Fantasy

9. Romance

10. Adventure and mystery

Chapter 14

OBJECTIVE SUMMARY

WHAT IS OBJECTIVE SUMMARY?

Say you just got into a water fight with your brother in the backyard. It started innocently enough. He asked for a glass of water, and you brought it over. But you tripped and spilled the water all over him. So he picked up the garden hose and doused you. Of course, you grabbed the garden hose and doused him.

THEN your mom arrives.

"WHAT HAPPENED?" she asks. "He's the biggest jerk in the world!" you might yell. "I didn't do anything!" your brother might yell back. Neither of you is giving her a **SUMMARY** that is **OBJECTIVE**.

> **SUMMARY**
> a brief account or review of something

An OBJECTIVE SUMMARY excludes personal views or attitudes. In contrast, a summary that is **SUBJECTIVE** is influenced by a person's perspective and/or feelings, not just the facts. Opinions can differ from person to person, while facts remain true no matter your perspective.

> **OBJECTIVE**
> without personal opinions or judgments

> **SUBJECTIVE**
> based on personal opinion

To save a life, this fireman needs information from an objective summary.

OPINION — FIRE IS PRETTY!

OPINION — I DON'T LIKE FIRES!

OPINION — BEING A FIREMAN IS COOL!

BUT IS THERE ANYONE IN THE BUILDING?

To write an objective summary is to PARAPHRASE or summarize a passage and express the same meaning.

Often, a paraphrase is briefer and clearer than the original language. Also, when you take all of the personal opinions and debatable judgments out of a statement, sometimes you discover there are only a handful of facts.

EXAMPLE:

I couldn't believe it! I never thought anything like this could happen in our neighborhood, but wouldn't you know, the instant I came around the corner, I could see smoke billowing from my neighbor's backyard. I bet it's an enemy warhead! Or a gas line explosion! Or you know what? It could be the smoking remains of an alien spaceship.

The only objective summary that you can make of this passage is that there was smoke coming from your neighbor's yard.

It's not just excited neighbors who offer a lot of personal opinions. Writers do it, too.

EXAMPLE:

In this selection from JAPANESE FAIRY TALES, Yei Theodora Ozaki relates the story of a farmer and a badger.

Long, long ago, there lived an old farmer and his wife who had made their home in the mountains, far from any town.

OPINION!

Their only neighbor was a bad and malicious badger. This badger used to come out every night and run across to the farmer's field and spoil the vegetables and the rice which the farmer spent his time in carefully cultivating. The badger

OPINION!

at last grew so ruthless in his mischievous work, and did so much harm everywhere on the farm, that the good-natured farmer could not stand it any longer, and determined to put a stop to it. So he lay in wait day after day and night after night, with a big club, hoping to catch the badger, but all in

OPINION!

vain. Then he laid traps for the wicked animal.

When we paraphrase, it's okay to state the opinions of the author and characters in the story. We just need to avoid adding OUR OWN opinions when we're writing an objective summary, otherwise our paraphrase becomes subjective.

SUBJECTIVE SUMMARY EXAMPLE:

Yei Theodora Ozaki thought that the badger who kept eating the farmer's crops was doing it just to bother the farmer, but I think the badger was hungry and needed something to eat.

PERSONAL OPINION! DOESN'T BELONG IN AN OBJECTIVE SUMMARY

OBJECTIVE SUMMARY EXAMPLE:

Yei Theodora Ozaki recorded a Japanese fairy tale about a farmer and a badger. She writes that the badger destroyed the farmer's crop and characterized the badger as malicious.

HOW to WRITE an OBJECTIVE SUMMARY

1. **STICK TO THE FACTS.** Is what you're writing a fact and NOT a judgment? If it's a personal judgment or opinion, leave it out!

2. **CHOOSE WHAT'S IMPORTANT.** Don't choose random facts; include only what matters most. If you don't need a fact to get the main point across, leave it out.

3. **PUT IT IN ORDER.** What's a clear way to explain what you just read? Start at the beginning, and make sure everything's in the right order, all the way to the end.

OFTEN CHRONOLOGICAL ORDER IS BEST, BUT NOT 100% OF THE TIME—SO YOU BE THE JUDGE!

4. **CHECK YOUR FACTS.** When you're done, check what you've written against what you've just read. Can you find a source for everything you've written? If not, leave it out!

I CAN'T FIND A SOURCE FOR ANYTHING I'VE JUST WRITTEN!

THEN YOUR SUMMARY IS PROBABLY NOT OBJECTIVE. BUT YOU SURE HAVE A LOT OF OPINIONS!

1. Fill in the blank:
   A paraphrase is usually briefer and _____ than the original text.

2. What is the opposite of subjective?

3. If something is free from personal opinion or judgment, is it objective or subjective?

4. What is another name for an objective summary?

5. Is the following sentence an objective summary?
   I didn't like any of the racers I saw at the track this weekend.

6. True or false: A personal opinion is your personal attitude or taste.

7. Is the following sentence an objective summary?
   The Declaration of Independence says that we were all created equal and we should all be free.

8. True or false: An objective summary should clearly state your own opinions.

9. Write a brief objective summary of "A Thirsty Pigeon" from AESOP'S FABLES:

A pigeon who was very thirsty saw a goblet of water painted on a signboard. Without stopping to see what it was, she flew to it with a loud whir, and dashing against the signboard, jarred herself terribly. Having broken her wings, she fell to the ground, and was caught by a man, who said, "Your zeal should never outrun your caution."

GOBLET NOW WITH EVEN MORE WATER!

10. Paraphrase "A Thirsty Crow" from AESOP'S FABLES:

A thirsty crow once spied a pitcher, and flew to it to see if by chance there was any water in it. When she looked in, she saw that there was water, but that it was so far from the top that she could not reach it, though she stretched her neck as far as she could. She stopped, and thought to herself, "How shall I get that water? I am perishing with thirst, and there must be some way for me to get some of it." Some pebbles were lying on the ground, and, picking them up in her beak, she dropped them one by one into the pitcher. They sank to the bottom, and at last the water was pushed up by them to the top, so that the Crow could easily drink it. "Where there's a will, there's a way," said the Crow.

CHECK YOUR ANSWERS

1. Clearer

2. Objective

3. Objective

4. Paraphrase

5. No

6. True

7. Yes

#9 and #10 have more than one correct answer.

8. False

9. A thirsty pigeon flew at a goblet of water painted on a sign and injured herself. The man who picked her up warned her not to let her zeal outrun her caution.

10. A thirsty crow dropped pebbles into a pitcher to raise the level of the water so she could drink it. The crow conveys the lesson "Where there's a will, there's a way."

Chapter 15

TEXTUAL ANALYSIS and EVIDENCE

WHAT IS TEXTUAL ANALYSIS and EVIDENCE?

TEXTUAL ANALYSIS is studying the **EVIDENCE** in a text to understand its meaning. TEXTUAL EVIDENCE is information in the text that backs up your **ANALYSIS**.

> **EVIDENCE**
> facts or information that prove something

There are two kinds of textual evidence—explicit and implicit. EXPLICIT EVIDENCE is proof plainly stated in the text.

> **ANALYSIS**
> a close examination of the parts or structure of something, usually as a basis for understanding, discussing, and interpreting it

↖ COMES RIGHT OUT AND SAYS IT

For instance, if your dad is upset because you didn't clean your room, he might tell you, "I'm annoyed that you didn't clean your room. I'm getting pretty tired of asking you to do it."

IMPLICIT EVIDENCE is evidence that is only implied by what is stated in the text. For example, if you come home and your dad is frowning and

YOU HAVE TO → FIGURE OUT WHAT THE AUTHOR IS SUGGESTING FROM THE TEXT.

stomping around the living room, you might guess that "Dad seems mad about something." That's implicit evidence that you could infer from.

EXAMPLE:

"In Our Neighborhood," by Alice Ruth Moore:

> The Harts were going to give a party. Neither Mrs. Hart, nor the Misses Hart, nor the small and busy Harts who amused themselves and the neighborhood by continually falling in the gutter on special occasions, had mentioned this fact to anyone, but all the interested denizens of that particular square could tell by the unusual air of bustle and activity which pervaded the Hart domicile.

Evidence and reason are closely related, but they're not the same. Evidence answers the question "What makes you think that?" Reason answers the question "Why is that important?"

The author doesn't include any discussion by the Hart family where they say, "We're having a party," so there is no explicit evidence of a party. However, the author writes that the neighbors are guessing there will be a party based on implicit evidence—they see the Harts preparing their house for a party.

INFERENCE
a conclusion we draw based on evidence and reason

When we make a guess based on implicit or explicit evidence, we're **DRAWING AN INFERENCE**.

EXAMPLE:

In DON QUIXOTE, Miguel Cervantes describes an old man who has read many adventure stories and decides to set out on an adventure of his own.

In short, his wits being quite gone, he hit upon the strangest notion that ever madman in this world hit upon, and that was that he fancied it was right and requisite, as well for the support of his own honour as for the service of his country, that he should make a knight-errant of himself, roaming the world over in full armour and on horseback in quest of adventures, and putting in practice himself all that he had read of as being the usual practices of knights-errant; righting every kind of wrong, and exposing himself to peril and danger from which, in the issue, he was to reap eternal renown and fame. Already the poor man saw himself crowned by the might of his arm Emperor of Trebizond at least; and so, led away by the intense enjoyment he found in these pleasant fancies, he set himself forthwith to put his scheme into execution.

The first thing he did was to clean up some armour that had belonged to his great-grandfather, and had been for ages lying forgotten in a corner eaten with rust and covered with mildew. He scoured and polished it as best he could, but he perceived one great defect in it, that it had no closed helmet, nothing but a simple morion. This deficiency, however, his ingenuity supplied, for he contrived a kind of half-helmet of pasteboard which, fitted on to the morion, looked like a whole one. It is true that, in order to see if it was strong and fit to stand a cut, he drew his sword and gave

IMPLICIT EVIDENCE

EXPLICIT EVIDENCE

it a couple of slashes, the first of which undid in an instant what had taken him a week to do. The ease with which he had knocked it to pieces disconcerted him somewhat, and to guard against that danger he set to work again, fixing bars of iron on the inside until he was satisfied with its strength; and then, **not caring to try any more experiments with it, he passed it and adopted it as a helmet of the most perfect construction.**

TO PARAPHRASE, the main character decides to become a knight-errant, or a medieval knight who searches for adventure. He imagines himself rewarded by kings for his deeds. To that end, he fixes up some old armor, but his repaired helmet doesn't stand up to a test. He adds iron to the helmet, but he does not test it again.

After reading this paragraph, you may draw the inference that Don Quixote is not qualified to be a knight-errant.

Some explicit evidence might be that he does not have the proper equipment. Some implicit evidence might be that he only knows what it's like to be a knight-errant from reading stories; the author is suggesting that Don Quixote doesn't have the real-life training he needs. We may also point to the implicit evidence that he determines his makeshift helmet "the most perfect construction" even though he has not tested it. The writer is implying that Don Quixote is perhaps not smart or thorough enough (or not sane enough!) to become a knight-errant.

HAVE AT YOU!

THE BEST EVIDENCE

Most texts are full of evidence. It's easy to pull out one piece—or more. But it's usually more useful to focus on the BEST evidence. When you are looking for the best evidence to support a deduction, ask yourself, "Would everyone agree that this evidence leads to my conclusion?"

EXAMPLE:

We want to prove that Don Quixote is not in his right mind. There are lots of pieces of evidence for this in the text:

> Don Quixote imagines that he should become a knight.

> He imagines kings will reward him.

> He imagines that he can use his grandfather's old armor on his adventures.

> He believes he can repair rusted and mildewy armor with pasteboard.

> He does not test the armor after he fixes it a second time.

However, we should choose the very best one. Which piece of evidence would everyone agree leads to the conclusion that Don Quixote is not in his right mind?

> Don Quixote imagines becoming a knight.

> He believes he can repair rusted and mildewy armor with pasteboard.

It's not so strange for Don Quixote to imagine becoming a knight. After all, most of us dream at some point that we might become a basketball star, a famous singer, or even the president. But most of us know that we can't repair medieval armor with pasteboard. Not knowing that makes Don Quixote seem out of touch with reality. It's the best evidence.

He does not test the armor after
he fixes it a second time.

He imagines kings will reward him.

Again, it's not too strange to hope that we might receive
praise from powerful people, even if it's unlikely that we
will. But not to test armor after you repair it is dangerous.
It could even be a matter of life and death. When Don
Quixote doesn't test his armor, we know he's not in his
right mind. It's the best evidence.

If we want to show someone is not in his right mind, we
choose evidence that everyone can agree shows him being
out of touch with reality.

CHECK YOUR KNOWLEDGE

1. If something is implicit, is it clearly stated?

2. If something is explicit, do we need to use reason to deduce it?

3. Read this passage from THE HOUSE BEHIND THE CEDARS, by Charles W. Chesnutt. What explicit evidence can you find to support the deduction that the dressmaker is skilled?

Rena placed herself unreservedly in the hands of Mrs. Newberry, who introduced her to the best dressmaker of the town, a woman of much experience in such affairs, who improvised during the afternoon a gown suited to the occasion. Mrs. Marshall had made more than a dozen ball dresses during the preceding month; being a wise woman and understanding her business thoroughly, she had made each one of them so that with a few additional touches it might serve for the Queen of Love and Beauty.

4. Read this passage from THE WINDY HILL, by Cornelia Meigs. What explicit evidence can you find to support the deduction that the room was dark?

> The place seemed very cheerless and empty after he had gone. The long windows gave little light on that gray winter afternoon, and the big fireplace with its glowing logs was at the far end of the room. There were shadows already on the shelves of heavy ledgers lining the walls, and on the rows of ship's models all up and down the sides of the big counting room.

5. What do we call it when we use reason to discover implicit evidence?

6. If your brother figures out that you wore his T-shirt because there is now a new big stain on it, has he used implicit or explicit evidence?

7. If you wanted to prove that someone was smart, would you write about how he or she aced a pop quiz, or how he or she aced the final exam?

8. You can tell your friend is happy because he is singing an upbeat song at the top of his lungs. Did you use explicit or implicit evidence?

9. You know your teacher is going to give a quiz whenever you come in and see "QUIZ" written on the board. Do you know this because of implicit or explicit evidence?

ANSWERS

CHECK YOUR ANSWERS

1. No

2. No

3. She is known as the best dressmaker in town.
   She has experience making dresses
   She can sew a dress in an afternoon.
   She has made a dozen dresses that month.
   She understands her business thoroughly.

4. The windows don't let in much light.
   The afternoon is not sunny.
   The fireplace is far away.
   Shadows were on the walls and objects in the room.

5. Making or drawing an inference

6. Implicit

#4 and #5 have more than one correct answer.

7. The final exam

8. Implicit

9. Explicit

Chapter 16

AUTHORSHIP AND NARRATION

WHAT IS an AUTHOR?

An **AUTHOR** is the person who wrote a book, article, poem, or other work.

AUTHOR BACKGROUND and PERSPECTIVE

Every author has a different biographical background. An author's biographical background is his or her life story and experiences.

IT INCLUDES:

* **CULTURE**

* historical period, or when the author was alive

* location

* personal experiences

> **CULTURE**
> the attitudes, knowledge, customs, beliefs, and objects that belong to a specific group of people

Depending on the time, place, and culture an author lived in, his or her point of view can be very different from another author. The author's biographical background can affect his or her perspective, or the way an author sees the world, and the way he or she writes. Once we understand an author's background, we can put his or her writing in that context.

> ↖ Once we understand who the author is, we can understand more about why he or she wrote the piece in the first place.

EXAMPLE:

There were two countries—*Blue* and *Red*. The country of Blue invaded the country of Red and won a huge victory. If a poet grew up in the country of Blue, what might his poem about the country of Blue be like? If a playwright grew up in the country of Red, what might her play be like if she wrote about the country of Blue?

The reader can analyze whether an author's biographical background affects his or her perspective in simple or more complex ways. Homer, the ancient Greek poet, couldn't write about cell phones, because he lived in a time before they were invented. But sometimes the way an author's biographical background affects his or her perspective is more complex. Jane Austen was an author at a time and place when women weren't allowed to hold many jobs. She couldn't write about a woman who was a doctor or a lawyer or a politician, because there weren't any during the time when she lived.

> YEAH...I'M WORKING ON THIS PRETTY EPIC POEM.

> WHICH IS WHY SCIENCE FICTION AUTHORS ARE SO CREATIVE—THEY OFTEN IMAGINE A FUTURE VERY DIFFERENT FROM OUR LIVES, WHICH IS REALLY HARD TO DO.

AUTHOR VS. NARRATOR

A **NARRATOR** is the character who relates the events of a story. It's NOT the same thing as an author. The narrator is a character that an author created. The narrator can be similar to or different from the author. In fiction texts, the narrator is a fictional creation of the author—just like any other character in the story.

EXAMPLE:

There are a lot of differences between the character of Huck Finn, who narrates THE ADVENTURES OF HUCKLEBERRY FINN, and the book's author, Mark Twain.

NARRATOR

Huck Finn
(a fictional person)

Is an orphan

Is a kid

Can't write standard English

Lives on the Mississippi

AUTHOR

Mark Twain
(a real person)

Is not an orphan

Is a grown man

Makes a living writing standard English

Lives in Connecticut

Differentiating between the author and narrator is the first step toward understanding more about fiction. Is the narrator reliable, meaning he or she always tells the truth and everything that he or she knows? Or is he or she an UNRELIABLE NARRATOR—someone who sometimes hides the truth? Similar to understanding who the author is, once we understand who the narrator is, we can understand more about the character and what the author is trying to achieve by using this narrator.

1. Does the time in which an author is born affect his or her biographical background?

2. What do we call the character who relates the events of a story?

3. Define "culture."

4. Why is it important to know about an author's biographical background?

5. Do a narrator and an author always have the same biographical background?

6. Which is the most likely title of a book written by a boy who grew up on a farm during a long drought?
   A CITY SUMMER
   THE LAST DROP OF WATER
   A YOUNG LADY'S DREAMS

7. Would two authors from different countries have different perspectives?

8. Is the narrator's perspective always the same as the author's?

9. If two authors are born in the same hometown, a hundred years apart, would they have the same perspective?

10. Read this passage from the beginning of MOBY DICK, by Herman Melville. Then, name the author and the narrator.

> Call me Ishmael. Some years ago—never mind how long precisely—having little or no money in my purse, and nothing particular to interest me on shore, I thought I would sail about a little and see the watery part of the world.

ANSWERS ▸

CHECK YOUR ANSWERS

1. Yes

2. Narrator

3. The collection of beliefs, attitudes, and customs of a specific group of people

4. Because an author's background affects his or her perspective, or the way he or she sees and writes about the world

5. No

6. THE LAST DROP OF WATER

7. Yes

8. No

9. No

10. Author: Herman Melville; narrator: Ishmael

Chapter 17

SETTING

WHAT IS SETTING?

In literature, the **SETTING** is the surroundings and time in which the events of a story take place.

EXAMPLES:

WAR AND PEACE, by Leo Tolstoy, is set in Russia during the Napoleonic Wars.

A CHRISTMAS CAROL, by Charles Dickens, is set in Victorian-era London.

THE WIZARD OF OZ, by L. Frank Baum, is set in the fictional land of Oz.

SETTINGS CAN INCLUDE INFORMATION ABOUT:

* Era or period
* Date and time of day
* Geographical location
* Weather and natural surroundings
* Immediate surroundings of a character
* Social conditions

HOW AUTHORS SET the SCENE

An author SETS THE SCENE, or creates the setting, by describing the things you, the reader, might experience if you were there: what you'd see, hear, feel—sometimes even what you might smell or taste. Authors may also describe what's happening in the world beyond the present moment in the story: where we are in time and what big events have just brought us to this moment.

EXAMPLE:

In this paragraph from ALICE'S ADVENTURES IN WONDERLAND, by Lewis Carroll, Alice has ducked down a rabbit hole to chase a mysterious white rabbit.

The rabbit hole went straight on like a tunnel for some way, and then dipped suddenly down, so suddenly that Alice had not a moment to think about stopping herself before she found herself falling down what seemed to be a very deep well.

Either the well was very deep, or she fell very slowly, for she had plenty of time as she went down to look about her, and to wonder what was going to happen next. First, she tried to look down and make out what she was coming to, but it was too dark to see anything: then she looked at the sides of the well, and noticed that they were filled with cupboards and book-shelves: here and there she saw maps and pictures hung upon pegs.

What we learn about the setting:

The rabbit hole is like a tunnel.
It suddenly dips into something like a well.
The "well" is deep.

Time appears to move slowly in this world.

It's too dark to see below.
The walls are actually shelves
filled with things.

The description of this setting builds slowly, adding one detail on another. We learn something more from each new sentence, and if one of the details were left out, the rest of the setting wouldn't make much sense. If we heard about the shelves and maps before we knew Alice was falling through a well, they'd just be hanging in thin air.

In poetry, writers also build a setting line by line.

> ### THE SETTING ANSWERS THE FOLLOWING THREE QUESTIONS:
>
> Where does the story takes place?
>
> When does the story takes place?
>
> What are the conditions like in this time and place?

EXAMPLE:

"I WANDERED LONELY AS A CLOUD," by William Wordsworth:

I wandered lonely as a cloud
That floats on high o'er vales and hills,
When all at once I saw a crowd, ← A crowd of what?
A host, of golden daffodils; ← Daffodils!
Beside the lake, beneath the trees, ← Where is the narrator?
By the lake, under trees.
Fluttering and dancing in the breeze.

Continuous as the stars that shine ← *Is it nighttime?*

And twinkle on the milky way,

They stretched in never-ending line ← *The daffodils stretch as far as the narrator can see.*

Along the margin of a bay: ← *Now, the narrator is beside a bay.*

Ten thousand saw I at a glance,

Tossing their heads in sprightly dance.

The waves beside them danced; but they ← *The ocean is nearby now.*

Out-did the sparkling waves in glee: ← *The ocean sparkles more in the sunshine, so it must be daytime.*

A poet could not but be gay,

In such a jocund company:

I gazed—and gazed—but little thought

What wealth the show to me had brought . . .

In each **STANZA**, the narrator imagines the perspective of a cloud and describes daffodils in different locations as though he is watching from the sky. In the first stanza they are by a lake under some trees. In the second stanza, they are beside a bay, and in the third stanza, they are on the seaside.

STANZA
a group of lines that compose the basic segment of a poem

Next, suddenly, we're someplace else.

For oft, when on my couch I lie ← Now we're at the narrator's house.
In vacant or in pensive mood, ← The setting could even be the narrator's mood.
They flash upon that inward eye ← Now we're inside the narrator's mind!
Which is the bliss of solitude;
And then my heart with pleasure fills,
And dances with the daffodils.

In the last stanza, the narrator takes us inside a home and even further inside his mind and emotions; however, the memory of the daffodils outside returns. The development of the setting changes the whole meaning of the poem. It moves the setting of the whole poem from taking place outside to inside the narrator's mind. The setting's development also changes the time in which the setting can take place— the poem seems at first like a single day, but the narrator tells us it is a memory that can be recalled whenever.

DAFFODILS

SAME SETTING, DIFFERENT DESCRIPTION

Different types of texts can portray the same setting very differently. Both of these stories are set at bedtime, but they're not at all the same.

EXAMPLES:

From PETER PAN, by J. M. Barrie:

On the night we speak of all the children were once more in bed. It happened to be Nana's evening off, and Mrs. Darling had bathed them and sung to them till one by one they had let go her hand and slid away into the land of sleep.

All were looking so safe and cosy that she smiled at her fears now and sat down tranquilly by the fire to sew.

It was something for Michael, who on his birthday was getting into shirts. The fire was warm, however, and the nursery dimly lit by three night-lights, and presently the sewing lay on Mrs. Darling's lap. Then her head nodded, oh, so gracefully. She was asleep. Look at the four of them, Wendy and Michael over there, John here, and Mrs. Darling by the fire.

From OLIVER TWIST, by Charles Dickens:

"Well! You have come here to be educated, and taught a useful trade," said the red-faced gentleman in the high chair.

"So you'll begin to pick oakum to-morrow morning at six o'clock," added the surly one in the white waistcoat.

For the combination of both these blessings in the one simple process of picking oakum, Oliver bowed low by the direction of the beadle, and was then hurried away to a large ward; where, on a rough, hard bed, he sobbed himself to sleep. What a novel illustration of the tender laws of England! They let the paupers go to sleep!

The bedtime settings are similar—but these texts tell very different stories:

Peter Pan	Oliver Twist
Peaceful	Hurried
Private—family only	Public—part of large ward
Comfortable bed	Rough, hard bed
Mother is there	No parents are there

Why would two authors show the same setting in such different ways? Because each author wants to emphasize different things. J. M. Barrie, the author of PETER PAN, wants to show how safe and peaceful life is for the Darling children at home. But Dickens, the author of OLIVER TWIST, wants to make a point about how hard the lives of poor children could be at the time, when they were forced to work instead of attend school.

CHECK YOUR KNOWLEDGE

1. Does a setting describe how something happens or where it happens?

2. In a story about a genie in a bottle who belongs to a prince who lives in a beautiful castle, what is the setting?

3. How does the last stanza of Wordsworth's poem "I WANDERED LONELY AS A CLOUD" change the setting of the poem?

4. True or false: The Darling family in PETER PAN had a similar experience at bedtime as the character Oliver Twist in OLIVER TWIST.

5. True or false: If two authors describe a similar setting, like visiting the ocean, they'll say pretty much the same things.

6. List three features that a setting can include.

7. True or false: Another word for setting is "surroundings."

8. True or false: The setting doesn't have much impact on a story.

9. True or false: If two stories are set in the same place, you can expect pretty similar things to happen.

10. Paraphrase the setting of the following passage from AT THE EARTH'S CORE, by Edgar Rice Burroughs:

> Together we stepped out to stand in silent contemplation of a landscape at once weird and beautiful. Before us a low and level shore stretched down to a silent sea. As far as the eye could reach the surface of the water was dotted with countless tiny isles— some of towering, barren, granitic rock—others resplendent in gorgeous trappings of tropical vegetation, myriad starred with the magnificent splendor of vivid blooms.

CHECK YOUR ANSWERS

1. Where it happens

2. The beautiful castle, and possibly inside the bottle

3. The setting moves from the real world to inside the author's mind.

4. False

5. False

6. Any three of the following: era or period, date, time of day, geographical location, weather, natural surroundings, immediate surroundings of a character, social conditions

7. True

8. False

9. False

10. The characters are standing on the shore of a silent ocean filled with many islands, some rock and some covered with vegetation.

↖ #10 has more than one correct answer.

Chapter 18

CHARACTER

WHAT IS a CHARACTER?

A **CHARACTER** is an individual in a story. If the story is a world, the characters are the population. Think about the story of Rumpelstiltskin, who helps a poor miller's daughter pretend to spin straw into gold and then demands her firstborn child in return. Rumpelstiltskin, the miller, the miller's daughter—even the firstborn child—they're all characters!

A story can be focused less on the action and more on the characters that perform the action or are affected by it. By learning to analyze and understand characters, we can better understand all the other elements of a story and the author's overall message.

ALL OF THE ELEMENTS OF A STORY ARE INTERCONNECTED.

TYPES of CHARACTERS
Central and Secondary Characters

A CENTRAL CHARACTER is one of the characters the story focuses on. A SECONDARY CHARACTER does not receive the most attention of the story.

EXAMPLE:

THE ODYSSEY focuses on the adventures of Odysseus, the central character. The people and creatures he meets along the way are the secondary characters.

Main Character, Protagonist, and Antagonist

The most important character in a story is called the MAIN CHARACTER. The main character can be a person, an animal, a supernatural object, and/or a mix of all these things— there are no limits on who the main character is. However, the main character is always the central focus of the story.

THIS IS THE CHARACTER YOU'RE USUALLY ROOTING FOR!

A PROTAGONIST is one of the leading figures in a story and often champions a cause in the book or works to solve the main conflict in the story.

An ANTAGONIST is a character who comes into conflict with the protagonist—he or she prevents the problem from being solved.

Sometimes the protagonist is the main character—but not always!

EXAMPLE:

In TO KILL A MOCKINGBIRD, by Harper Lee, the main character is Scout. Most of the story is about her and what she thinks and feels. However, many readers believe that Atticus, her father, is the protagonist. He's the one we root for in the conflict of the story.

Lots of people think of the protagonist as the good guy and the antagonist as the bad guy, but these characters are often more complex than good versus bad. These characters are ways for the author to explore the complexity of a conflict and ways for the readers to discuss and analyze the story.

However, often the protagonist and the main character are the same.

EXAMPLE:

In the HARRY POTTER series, by J. K. Rowling, Harry is the protagonist and the main character. In the books, we follow Harry from the moment he learns he's a wizard on his eleventh birthday to a climactic battle with the series' antagonist, Lord Voldemort (or, He-Who-Must-Not-Be-Named).

Flat and Round Characters

A FLAT CHARACTER is one who can be summed up in just a few lines without many details about their beliefs, feelings, or behaviors. A ROUND CHARACTER is one who has a lot of depth and detail—more like a real person.

> The writer E. M. Forster came up with the idea of flat and round characters in his lecture series called **ASPECTS OF THE NOVEL.**

EXAMPLE:

The Wicked Witch of the West is a flat character in THE WIZARD OF OZ. We never learn much about her or why she acts the way she does. But in the novel and the musical WICKED, she is a round character. We learn a lot about her story and her feelings.

I HAVE FEELINGS, TOO!

> Sometimes we see the same character over and over again: the wise old lady, the trusted friend. These are called **STOCK CHARACTERS.**

Sympathetic and Unsympathetic Characters

A SYMPATHETIC CHARACTER is one we can relate to. An UNSYMPATHETIC CHARACTER is one we don't have much **SYMPATHY** for.

> **SYMPATHY**
> understanding between people; a common feeling; care

EXAMPLE:

Most of us would probably be sympathetic to a character who was on a mission to rescue puppies. Most of us would feel unsympathetic toward a character who wanted to steal a family's new puppy.

Each reader may have different feelings about different characters depending on his or her own feelings and background.

Dynamic and Static Characters

A DYNAMIC CHARACTER is one who changes during the course of a story. A STATIC CHARACTER doesn't change. Those changes can be physical, emotional, or spiritual, like growing up, falling in love, or finding hope after a tragedy.

EXAMPLE:

Wendy is a dynamic character in the play PETER PAN; OR THE BOY WHO WOULDN'T GROW UP. She learns and grows up. But Peter Pan is a static character, because no matter what happens, he doesn't learn or change.

DYNAMIC CHARACTER

STATIC CHARACTER

CHARACTER SUMMARY CHART

TYPES OF CHARACTERS	THIS CHARACTER . . .
CENTRAL	Is the most important character in the story; central to the action
SECONDARY	Appears in the story but is not the main focus
PROTAGONIST	Is a leading figure; the champion of the story
ANTAGONIST	Comes into conflict with the protagonist
FLAT	Has little depth and little information on beliefs, feelings, or behavior
ROUND	Has depth, like a real person
SYMPATHETIC	Is relatable
UNSYMPATHETIC	Is not relatable
DYNAMIC	Changes throughout the story
STATIC	Stays the same throughout the story

DISCLAIMER: THESE AREN'T THE **ONLY** KINDS OF CHARACTERS. THANKS TO GREAT WRITERS, THERE ARE MANY MORE!

Narrator as Character

The narrator tells the story, but sometimes the narrator is also a character who acts IN the story.

EXAMPLE:

Ishmael is the narrator in MOBY DICK. However, he's also a character who experiences the whole story of chasing a great white whale through the ocean. He's not the main character in the action of the story, but he tells the tale.

NARRATION and POINT of VIEW

In a narrative, the POINT OF VIEW is the perspective from which a story is told. If it's a fictional story, it is told from the point of view of the narrator. There are three common types of narrators in fiction:

1. A FIRST-PERSON NARRATOR is a narrator who is also a character in the story and tells it from his or her point of view. A first-person narrator tells the story in the FIRST PERSON and always refers to that character as "I" —or "WE," if it is plural.

Authors might choose to use first person if they want the story to be told from a single point of view and if the thoughts and feelings of the narrator are important to the story.

EXAMPLE:

I was born in a small mountain town called Della Gloria.

2. A SECOND-PERSON NARRATOR tells the story as if it is happening to "you," using words like "you" and "yours." Authors might choose second-person narration if they want the reader to strongly relate to the story or they are giving the reader specific instructions.

EXAMPLE:

You've probably never seen any place quite as beautiful as the serene mountain town of Della Gloria.

3. A THIRD-PERSON NARRATOR is a narrator who is not a character in the story. This narrator tells the story in the THIRD PERSON and refers to the characters as "**HE**," "**SHE**," and "**THEY**," but never "I" or "we."

A third-person narrator may have a limited point of view or be OMNISCIENT, which means the narrator knows all and can describe the points of view of many characters. An author might choose this point of view if she wanted to write about the points of view of many characters or tell the story without focusing much attention on the narrator.

EXAMPLE:

Sebastian Smith was proud to have been born in the small mountain town of Della Gloria. His older sister, Jacobia, was not.

A character's point of view is his or her perspective, or how a character sees and thinks about things. An author can develop or show a character's point of view in several different ways:

What the character DOES:

Janet offers Jimmy a bowl of ice cream. He refuses to eat it.

What the character says DIRECTLY:

Jimmy says, "I hate ice cream!"

But not all characters mean what they say! It's also important to watch what a character does. Also pay close attention to moments when a character's actions contradict his or her words, and vice versa.

What the character says or expresses INDIRECTLY: Janet offers Jimmy a glass of cold water, and he fishes all the ice out before he'll drink it.

Perhaps Jimmy doesn't like anything that's cold!

What other characters say and do in relation to the character: Janet says, "Oh! I forgot that your teeth are sensitive to the cold."

CONTRASTING CHARACTERS

One way a writer develops characters is to contrast them so the reader can see their differences and define them more clearly.

EXAMPLE:

Amy is a very protective character. She may not have much reason to show that . . . unless the author introduces Jessica, who tries to bully Amy's friend Talia. Suddenly Amy has someone to protect and someone to stand up to. If Jessica weren't mean to Talia, we might never learn how protective Amy is. Amy's protective qualities also highlight Jessica's aggressiveness.

Will Jessica back down if she's challenged? Will she learn something and be nicer after Amy stands up to her? Unless Amy and Jessica contrast each other, we might never find out about either of them!

Contrasting Characters to Create Effects

Sometimes authors contrast two characters to create an effect, or a certain feeling or mood, in a story.

HUMOR

Bob and Jason get stuck in a tiny cable car that is traveling on wires above an amusement park. Bob is terrified of heights and can't wait to get down, but Jason is totally comfortable and begins to spread out a lavish lunch from provisions in his backpack.

The author creates the contrasts in their reactions to make the scene funny. This is a classic odd-couple pairing that we read often and see a lot of in film, theater, and television.

SUSPENSE

Candace and Marie live next door to each other. Candace keeps her place incredibly neat, and Marie's place is always a mess. When Candace has to go out of town for a week, she asks Marie to come over a few times, just to water her plants. But Marie decides the plants must be lonely, so she spends hours over at Candace's place while Candace is gone—and makes the place a total mess. Before Marie has a chance to clean up, Candace decides to come home early!

How will Candace react when she gets home? The author creates a large contrast between their two attitudes on the meaning of "clean" to create suspense.

CHARACTER and PLOT CHANGE

Another way we learn things about characters is through PLOT, or the sequence of events in a story. A PLOT CHANGE (sometimes called a PLOT TWIST) is a sudden change in the events of a story from what is to be expected. ← A SURPRISE!
An author can use a plot change to reveal characteristics about each character by showing how the characters react differently to the event.

EXAMPLE:

There are two characters: Christine and Laura. They both live on the same block, attend the same school, and love science. But then

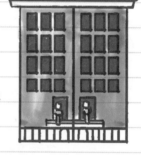

THIS IS THE PLOT CHANGE. → a spaceship crashes on the edge of town, and residents begin to come down with a mysterious disease. Laura is terrified. She decides to stay home so she doesn't get sick. But Christine wants to help.
She works in the biology lab at school and helps discover a cure.

Until the plot changes, Laura and Christine seem to be the same. But after the plot change, we can see that they're actually very different.

SIMILAR CHARACTERS, DIFFERENT STORIES

Different types of texts may include similar characters. However, because of the traditions of a particular genre, the characters come across differently. We can compare and contrast similar characters to explore the different texts.

EXAMPLE:

The main character in Charlotte Brontë's JANE EYRE is an orphan named Jane Eyre. Similarly, Mary Lennox is an orphan in Frances Hodgson Burnett's THE SECRET GARDEN. Both books tell a coming-of-age story. However, the books come from different genres—JANE EYRE is mix of a mystery and a romance novel, while THE SECRET GARDEN is a young adult novel. When we compare and contrast the characters, we can see how the genres encourage different characters: Jane lives in a gothic manor, gets involved with a dark mystery with lots of suspense, has dreams where she sees the future, and falls in love. Mary also a lives in a manor full of secrets, where she discovers a family member she never knew she had. The cousin is ill, but she nurses him back to health and they build a strong friendship while exploring the manor's garden.

Excerpt from Charlotte Brontë's JANE EYRE:

> There was no possibility of taking a walk that day. We had been wandering, indeed, in the leafless shrubbery an hour in the morning; but since dinner (Mrs. Reed, when there was no company, dined early) the cold winter wind had brought with it clouds so sombre, and a rain so penetrating, that further out-door exercise was now out of the question.
>
> I was glad of it: I never liked long walks, especially on chilly afternoons: dreadful to me was the coming home in the raw twilight, with nipped fingers and toes, and a heart saddened by the chidings of Bessie, the nurse, and humbled by the consciousness of my physical inferiority to Eliza, John, and Georgiana Reed.

Excerpt from Frances Hodgson Burnett's THE SECRET GARDEN:

When Mary Lennox was sent to Misselthwaite Manor to live with her uncle everybody said she was the most disagreeable-looking child ever seen. It was true, too. She had a little thin face and a little thin body, thin light hair and a sour expression. Her hair was yellow, and her face was yellow because she had been born in India and had always been ill in one way or another. Her father had held a position under the English Government and had always been busy and ill himself, and her mother had been a great beauty who cared only to go to parties and amuse herself with gay people. She had not wanted a little girl at all, and when Mary was born she handed her over to the care of an Ayah, who was made to understand that if she wished to please the Mem Sahib she must keep the child out of sight as much as possible. So when she was a sickly, fretful, ugly little baby she was kept out of the way, and when she became a sickly, fretful, toddling thing she was kept out of the way also. She never remembered seeing familiarly anything but the dark faces of her Ayah and the other native servants, and as they always obeyed her and gave her her own way in everything, because the Mem Sahib would be angry if she was disturbed by her crying, by the time she was six years old she was as tyrannical and selfish a little pig as ever lived. The young English governess who came to teach her to read and write disliked her so much that she gave up her place in three months, and when other governesses came to try to fill it they always went away in a shorter time than the first one. So if Mary had not chosen to really want to know how to read books she would never have learned her letters at all.

COMPARISONS

Both characters are:

* young

* girls

* orphans

* living with people who are not their own families

* living in England

* not considered pretty

* opinionated

CONTRASTS

Jane Eyre

* a sense of dread

* grew up with modest means

* does not live a fancy lifestyle

* is not used to getting her own way

Mary Lennox

* no fears of others

* grew up rich

* lives a fancy lifestyle

* is used to getting her own way

CHECK YOUR KNOWLEDGE

1. What do we call any actor in a story?

2. Does a static character learn anything during the course of a story?

3. How can changes in plot help us learn anything about or develop a character?

4. Will every reader find the same characters sympathetic and unsympathetic?

5. How can we learn something about a character's point of view by the things he does?

6. Can a character in a story also be the story's narrator?

7. True or false: We never learn more about a character based on their reactions to another character.

8. True or false: E. M. Forster first described the idea of protagonists and antagonists.

9. True or false: An antagonist doesn't come into conflict with the protagonist of a story.

10. Compare and contrast the characters in this passage from JANET: A TWIN, by Dorothy Whitehill:

> A long snake settled into the road, a wiry little Irish terrier bounded after it, followed by a whirling fury of starched petticoats, long slender legs and an immense red bow.
>
> This was Janet.
>
> A tiny cloud of dust curtained them all for a minute; when it settled, it disclosed a rigid tableau. Janet held the dog's collar in one strong little brown hand, and with the other and the aid of one foot she grasped the snake.
>
> "Do something!" she demanded excitedly, as she turned angry eyes toward a fat, roly-poly figure that still remained partially hidden by the scrub oak, watching the scene with an expression of fear and distaste in his pale blue eyes.
>
> This was Harry Waters.

ANSWERS

CHECK YOUR ANSWERS

1. A character

2. No

3. When the plot changes, we discover how a character reacts.

4. No

5. The things a character does can reveal what he thinks and feels.

6. Yes

7. False

8. False. Forster introduced flat and round characters.

9. False

10. Janet takes action. She is adventurous, commanding, and not afraid of snakes. Harry is fearful and does not like snakes.

#10 has more than one correct answer.

Chapter 19

PLOT

WHAT IS PLOT?

The plot, or the sequence of events in a story, creates action. The actions in a story build **DRAMA**. All that action and drama usually works toward a **RESOLUTION**. When an author creates a plot, he or she is creating a chain reaction—there are causes and effects to the action. There are an infinite number of **PLOTLINES** that an author can create—what he or she creates can reveal the meaning and message behind the story.

kids conquering a monster

kids becoming wealthy

kids on a sailboat

kids laughing

kids with a medal looking worn out and proud

kids consoling one another

kids climbing a castle

Almost all plots follow this basic sequence, which was first described by the German novelist and playwright GUSTAV FREYTAG and is sometimes described as FREYTAG'S PYRAMID.

1. **EXPOSITION**: The author sets the scene and explains what's going on.

2. **RISING ACTION**: a series of crises that lead to the climax

3. **CLIMAX**: the most exciting moment of a story, where both people and events change

4. **FALLING ACTION**: the events that follow the climax

5. **RESOLUTION**: the conclusion, in which all the tensions of the plot are resolved

PLOT the sequence of events in a story that together create action and build drama

Climax
the most exciting moment of a story, where both people and events change

Rising Action
a series of crises that lead to the climax

Falling Action
the events that follow the climax

FREYTAG'S PYRAMID

Exposition
The author sets the scene and explains what's going on.

Resolution
the conclusion, in which all the tensions of the plot are resolved

CLASSIC PLOTS

There are all kinds of plots, but there are some big patterns you'll see over and over again. Classic plots are stories that have the same basic sequence of events and appear in many stories throughout history. Classic plots can come from:

MYTHS FROM AROUND THE WORLD

TRADITIONAL STORIES, such as fairy tales and folktales like the ones collected by the Brothers Grimm or invented by Hans Christian Andersen.

RELIGIOUS WORKS FROM SACRED TEXTS

Other sources, like **HARDBOILED NOVELS**, **ADVENTURES**, or **ROMANCES**, where many authors tell the same basic story with different details.

EXAMPLE:

A plot about the children from warring families who happen to fall in love has been repeated:

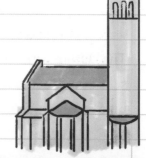

Traditional version: ROMEO AND JULIET is a play by William Shakespeare set in medieval Verona and Mantua in Italy.

Modern version:
WEST SIDE STORY is an American musical based on ROMEO AND JULIET. Instead of the star-crossed lovers being torn between warring Italian families, they're torn between warring New York City gangs.

EXAMPLE:

The plot about a brave upstart who stands up to a much stronger enemy and wins has reappeared:

Religious version: In the biblical story of David and Goliath, David, a young Israelite, stands up to the giant Goliath. Using only a slingshot and a stone, he brings him down.

Modern version: In the movie MR. SMITH GOES TO WASHINGTON, a young congressman stands up to much more powerful politicians and defeats them.

EXAMPLE:

The plot about an artist who creates an image of a woman and then falls in love with the image he made has been reused:

Mythological version: In Ovid's poem METAMORPHOSES, a sculptor falls in love with a statue he carved.

Modern version: In the musical MY FAIR LADY, a rich man helps a young lady from the streets become his ideal of the perfect woman, then falls in love with her.

HOW an AUTHOR CREATES a PLOT

OR STANZAS, IF THE STORY IS TOLD IN A POEM!

An author composes a plot piece by piece with **SCENES**. Scenes make up the story, including all the pieces of plot: exposition, rising action, climax, falling action, and resolution. You can chart the plot of a story you read (or build your own story) by creating a PLOT DIAGRAM (similar to the plot pyramid, and sometimes called **STORYBOARDING**). A plot diagram shows the plot of a story, scene by scene or plot section by plot section.

> **SCENE**
> an individual event in a story

> **STORYBOARDING**
> creating a series of drawings that represent a plot

214

EXAMPLE:

An Indian fairy tale, retold by Joseph Jacobs, shows how three different scenes create a plot.

1ST SCENE

2ND SCENE

3RD SCENE

TEXT →

ONCE THERE LIVED a great Raja, whose name was Salabhan, and he had a Queen, by name Lona, who, though she wept and prayed at many a shrine, had never a child to gladden her eyes. After a long time, however, a son was promised to her.

Queen Lona returned to the palace, and when the time for the birth of the promised son drew nigh, she inquired of three Jogis who came begging to her gate, what the child's fate would be, and the youngest of them answered and said, "Oh, Queen! the child will be a boy, and he will live to be a great man. But for twelve years you must not look upon his face, for if either you or his father see it before the twelve years are past, you will surely die! This is what you must do; as soon as the child is born you must send him away to a cellar underneath the ground, and never let him see the light of day for twelve years. After they are over, he may come forth, bathe in the river, put on new clothes, and visit you. His name shall be Raja Rasalu, and he shall be known far and wide."

So, when a fair young Prince was in due time born into the world, his parents hid him away in an underground palace, with nurses, and servants, and everything else a King's son might desire.

In the FIRST scene, the queen prays at a shrine for a son. From the sentences, we can see that the queen doesn't have a son, wants a son, and a son is promised to her. This propels the plot forward by setting up the conflict of the story: The queen wants a son and doesn't have one.

PEOPLE WHO ARE MASTERS AT YOGA →

In the SECOND scene, the queen meets with Jogis (or yogis) at the palace gate. They make a prediction that she will die if she sees her son during his first 12 years and give her instructions on how to avoid this fate. This propels the story forward by ensuring that there is conflict after the child is born, because the king and queen can't just have a normal life with him.

In the LAST scene, the young prince is born and hidden away. He is put in an underground palace with servants. This propels the story forward by building curiosity, and possible conflict, over what in the world will happen when the young prince comes out of hiding.

The writer may have planned the plot with a plot pyramid, like so:

Climax

Perhaps the boy's twelfth birthday or an early escape ...

Rising Action

A son is promised, but the yogis tell her she must hide the son away until his twelfth birthday, or all will die. So, the son is hidden away.

Falling Action

Exposition

There is a king and queen who want a son.

Resolution

Each scene propels the plot forward to the climax, which could be the boy's twelfth birthday or an early escape. The consequences that unfold thereafter are the falling action and resolution.

Other Parts of Plot

Scenes build the structure of a story, but this fairy tale contains other elements of plot, like:

CHARACTERS: Plot is what happens to the characters in a story, but who a character is also affects the plot.

EXAMPLE:

> The queen in the Indian folktale seems to believe what the yogis said to her. But imagine if she had been stubborn instead: What if she had refused to do what the yogis said? This might be a very different story!

DIALOGUE: It may not seem like we're doing much when we talk. But the things people say can make other people mad, make two people fall in love, make them spill state secrets, and more.

> **DIALOGUE**
> things that characters say to one another in a story

EXAMPLE:

> In the folktale, the yogis don't have an army to force the king and queen to do what they say. But their simple words inspire the king and queen to hide their own son away for 12 whole years.

DESCRIPTION: What we think about a person or a place affects the way we feel about it and what we might do.

> **DESCRIPTION**
> language that tells the reader how things are, look, sound, or feel

EXAMPLE:

Imagine if the underground palace where the boy is hidden was described as "dank and dark." That might be enough to make his mother, or his father, or somebody else who cared about him want to get him out of there.

HOUSE

BEAUTIFUL HOUSE

HAUNTED HOUSE

CHECK YOUR KNOWLEDGE

1. What do we call the way events are structured to create a story?

2. Does rising action happen before or after falling action?

3. Can a character's laziness change the plot of a story?

4. Does a story's setting affect the plot?

5. What do we call one of the main events in a story?

6. What do we call the things people say to one another in a story?

7. What is at the peak of a plot pyramid?

8. What do we call the part of a story where the conflict is settled?

9. Can something as small as a single sentence affect the course of a whole plot?

10. Draw a plot diagram for this story:

A poor young farmer named Jack spends all his family money on some magic beans. His mother is furious, but when he plants them, a giant beanstalk grows. He climbs it to the sky, where the rich giant who lives there threatens to eat him. But Jack escapes and hurries back down the beanstalk. When the giant tries to chase Jack back to earth, Jack chops down the beanstalk, killing the giant. He and his mother live happily ever after on the giant's riches.

ANSWERS

1. Plot

2. Before

3. Yes

4. Yes

5. Scene

6. Dialogue

7. The climax

8. Resolution

9. Yes

10. →

Climax
Jack chops down beanstalk.

Rising Action
Jack buys beans, climbs beanstalk, meets giant, and flees giant.

Falling Action
Giant dies.

Exposition
Jack and his family have no money.

Resolution
Jack and his mother are rich.

Chapter 20

THEME

WHAT IS a THEME?

A THEME is the unifying idea in a piece of writing. It's not the topic, but rather how the author approaches the topic. Often it's what the narrator and characters are wrestling with for the whole story. A theme isn't just one part of a story or poem, like a piece of pie you can slice out and give to someone. It's more like an ingredient that affects the whole passage: like adding hot sauce in chili. When you mix hot sauce into chili, it affects everything in the soup—everything gets hot! The same thing is true with the theme.

You find evidence of theme in all the other elements of the story, including:

the characters

the setting

the plot

Topic Versus Theme

Two pieces of writing may be about the topic of courage, but they may have different themes.

EXAMPLE: With the topic of courage, different authors can write on different themes.

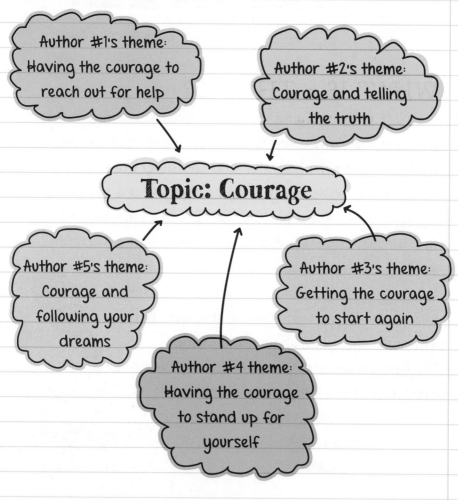

Author #1's theme: Having the courage to reach out for help

Author #2's theme: Courage and telling the truth

Topic: Courage

Author #5's theme: Courage and following your dreams

Author #4 theme: Having the courage to stand up for yourself

Author #3's theme: Getting the courage to start again

Classic Themes

YOU CAN HAVE MORE THAN ONE THEME IN A BOOK.

There are all kinds of themes in stories and poems, but here are some of the big ones you'll see over and over again:

The Importance of Love and Friendship

EXAMPLE: In J.R.R. Tolkien's LORD OF THE RINGS, evil is vanquished only when a friend helps a friend.

Dealing with Loss

EXAMPLE: In Frances Hodgson Burnett's THE SECRET GARDEN, Mary Lennox has to learn to deal with the loss of both of her parents.

The Importance of Family

EXAMPLE: In Madeleine L'Engle's A WRINKLE IN TIME, it is the love Meg and her brother Charles Wallace have for their missing father that gives them the courage to journey through time and space to find him.

Learning to Be a Hero

EXAMPLE: In Greek mythology, Hercules has to perform 12 heroic labors, or tasks, to appease the gods.

What It Means to Grow Up

EXAMPLE: In PURPLE HIBISCUS, by Chimamanda Adichie, a teenage girl has to learn to become a grown, confident woman despite the difficulties her family faces.

The Coexistence of Good and Bad in a Person/the World

EXAMPLE: In Harper Lee's TO KILL A MOCKINGBIRD, a young girl watches as her father fights for justice in a small town.

Where Do You Find the Theme?

You find hints of the theme everywhere in a story:

IN THE DETAILS:

The theme doesn't show up in just one place; it'll come back up again and again, in the details of a story.

IN SENTENCES AND IN SCENES:

A single sentence can bring up a theme. A whole scene can be about it, too.

IN THE CHARACTERS:

A theme can appear in how a character changes. The way a main character evolves in response to a conflict often points to the theme.

ALL THE WAY THROUGH:

A theme will appear throughout a story, everywhere from the beginning to the end—sometimes in large ways, like a scene with a plot twist, and sometimes in detailed ways, like in the language used in a sentence.

EXAMPLE:

F. Scott Fitzgerald's THE DIAMOND AS BIG AS THE RITZ revolves around the topic of money and includes a few themes, but this passage focuses on the theme of how wealth categorizes people, as well as a theme of belonging and wealth.

Theme in the setting: The author immediately tells us that the narrator is wealthy by describing the distance driven in an expensive car!

Theme in the setting: Everyone is expected to drive expensive cars, so everyone in the setting is rich. The narrator is signaling that if the character doesn't drive a Rolls-Pierce, he or she don't belong.

St. Midas's School is half an hour from Boston in a Rolls-Pierce motor-car. The actual distance will never be known, for no one, except John T. Unger, had ever arrived there save in a Rolls-Pierce and probably no one ever will again. St. Midas's is the most expensive and the most exclusive boys' preparatory school in the world.

Theme in the setting: The people who go to this school must have a lot of money. It also must be a small amount of people who can afford this, because the author calls it "exclusive."

John's first two years there passed pleasantly. The fathers of all the boys were money-kings, and John spent his summers visiting at fashionable resorts.

Theme in the character: The fathers are described according to their relationship with money—not according to other characteristics, like if they are fun, smart, or creative.

Theme in the character: Everyone is the same. If the character is not the same—he or she don't belong.

While he was very fond of all the boys he visited, their fathers struck him as being much of a piece, and in his boyish way he often wondered at their exceeding sameness. When he told them where his home was they would ask jovially, "Pretty hot down there?" and John would muster a faint smile and answer, "It certainly is." His response would have been heartier had they not all made this joke—at best varying it with, "Is it hot enough for you down there?" which he hated just as much.

In the middle of his second year at school, a quiet, handsome boy named Percy Washington had been put in John's form. The new-comer was pleasant in his manner and exceedingly well dressed even for St. Midas's, but for some reason he kept aloof from the other boys. The only person with whom he was intimate was John T. Unger, but even to John he was entirely uncommunicative concerning his home or his family. That he was wealthy went without saying, but beyond a few such deductions John knew little of his friend, so it promised rich confectionery for his curiosity when Percy invited him to spend the summer at his home "in the West." He accepted, without hesitation.

Theme in the plot: The first big surprise in the plot is related to levels of wealth.

It was only when they were in the train that Percy became, for the first time, rather communicative. One day while they were eating lunch in the dining-car and discussing the imperfect characters of several of the boys at school, Percy suddenly changed his tone and made an abrupt remark.

"My father," he said, "is by far the richest man in the world."

SAME THEME, DIFFERENT TEXTS

However, just because two pieces of writing share a theme doesn't mean they express the theme the same way.

EXAMPLE:

This excerpt from A CHRISTMAS CAROL, by Charles Dickens, also revolves around the topic of money and has a theme about wealth categorizing people.

"A merry Christmas, uncle! God save you!" cried a cheerful voice. It was the voice of Scrooge's nephew, who came upon him so quickly that this was the first intimation he had of his approach.

"Bah!" said Scrooge, "Humbug!"

He had so heated himself with rapid walking in the fog and frost, this nephew of Scrooge's, that he was all in a glow; his face was ruddy and handsome; his eyes sparkled, and his breath smoked again.

"Christmas a humbug, uncle!" said Scrooge's nephew. "You don't mean that, I am sure?"

"I do," said Scrooge. "Merry Christmas! What right have you to be merry? What reason have you to be merry? You're poor enough."

"Come, then," returned the nephew gaily. "What right have you to be dismal? What reason have you to be morose? You're rich enough."

Dickens connects the idea of being rich with being happy. So far, two categories of people have emerged: wealthy and happy people, and poor and unhappy people.

Dickens connects being a poor person with being unhappy.

Dickens uses Scrooge's character to contradict the idea that being rich makes you happy.

Scrooge having no better answer ready on the spur of the moment, said "Bah!" again; and followed it up with "Humbug."

Dickens uses the nephew's character to contradict the idea that being poor makes you unhappy.

→ "Don't be cross, uncle!" said the nephew.

"What else can I be," returned the uncle, "when I live in such a world of fools as this? Merry Christmas! Out upon merry Christmas! What's Christmas time to you but a time for paying bills without *money*; a time for finding yourself a year older, but not an hour richer; a time for balancing your books and having every item in 'em through a round dozen of months presented dead against you? If I could work my will," said Scrooge indignantly, "every idiot who goes about with 'Merry Christmas' on his lips, should be boiled with his own pudding, and buried with a stake of holly through his heart. He should!"

Scrooge relates that everything in life is about money.

The character of Scrooge thinks being friendly and wishing friends and family "Merry Christmas" is a waste of time—he thinks you can better spend your time getting rich.

Both stories revolve around the themes of wealth and categories of people, but the authors express the theme in very different ways. We can <u>compare and contrast</u> how the two authors treat the topic of money through the theme:

THE DIAMOND AS BIG AS THE RITZ

Money is connected with positive things.

People with money are the same.

Money seems to increase freedom.

Money seems mysterious.

Money is inherited.

A CHRISTMAS CAROL

Money is connected with negative things.

People with money are grouchy.

Money seems to diminish freedom.

Money seems businesslike.

Money is made.

This acrostic summarizes all the important points about theme:

Theme: The subject, or big idea, in a piece of writing

How is a theme woven into a story?
- Through individual sentences, details, and words
- Through plot
- Through setting
- Through characters and character development

Engages with other aspects of the story:
- Theme impacts plot and characters (and vice versa).
- Plot and characters always relate to and engage with the theme.

Many themes are possible:
- Love and friendship
- Loss
- The importance of family
- Learning to be a hero
- Growing up
- Justice and injustice

Examine these questions to find the themes:
- What topic/big question are the characters in this story struggling with?
- How do different scenes in this story convey the same theme?
- What details does the author use to represent the theme?

CHECK YOUR KNOWLEDGE

1. What is a theme in a story?

2. Can you find evidence of a theme in something as small as a sentence?

3. Can a whole scene be about a theme?

4. True or false: A character will sometimes be described based on their relationship to a theme.

5. True or false: The setting of a story can contribute to the theme.

6. True or false: You can't find the theme by looking at the details.

7. True or false: A theme doesn't affect the plot.

8. True or false: Every story that's about the same theme will explore that theme the same way.

9. Read this passage from A ROOM WITH A VIEW, by E. M. Forster. What is the theme?

> One of the ill-bred people whom one does meet abroad leant forward over the table and actually intruded into their argument. He said: "I have a view, I have a view."
>
> Miss Bartlett was startled. Generally at a pension people looked them over for a day or two before speaking, and often did not find out that they would "do" till they had gone. She knew that the intruder was ill-bred, even before she glanced at him.

10. Read this opening passage from FRANKENSTEIN, OR THE MODERN PROMETHEUS, by Mary Wollstonecraft Shelley. What is the theme?

St. Petersburgh, Dec. 11th, 17—

TO Mrs. Saville, England

You will rejoice to hear that no disaster has accompanied the commencement of an enterprise which you have regarded with such evil forebodings. I arrived here yesterday, and my first task is to assure my dear sister of my welfare and increasing confidence in the success of my undertaking.

I am already far north of London, and as I walk in the streets of Petersburgh, I feel a cold northern breeze play upon my cheeks, which braces my nerves and fills me with delight. Do you understand this feeling? This breeze, which has travelled from the regions towards which I am advancing, gives me a foretaste of those icy climes. Inspirited by this wind of promise, my daydreams become more fervent and vivid.

CHECK YOUR ANSWERS

1. The subject or big idea in a piece of writing

2. Yes

3. Yes

4. True

5. True

6. False

7. False

8. False

9. Manners and perceptions of people

10. Ignoring warnings and being naive

#9 and #10 have more than one correct answer.

Chapter 21

TONE

WHAT IS TONE?

In literature, **TONE** is the way an author creates an attitude or mood in a piece of writing. You've probably heard someone say, "Watch your tone!" If you know what that means, you know what tone is.

EXAMPLE:

Say you don't want to go with your dad to the grocery store. There are a lot of different ways you can convey that information to him:

With a polite tone: "I'm sorry, Dad, I'd rather not."

With a whiny tone: "Why do I always have to go to the store with you?"

With an angry tone: "I'm not going to the store again!"

Some common examples of tone are:

Optimistic

Hurt

Compassionate

Agitated

Questioning

Authoritative

Hopeful

Nervous

... and on and on! There are countless tones an author can use. Also, tone can change throughout a story, depending on the scene, the drama, and the characters.

By understanding the tone of a piece of writing, you can gain a deeper understanding of all the elements of the story. In fact, a writer's purpose for writing may be revealed in the tone—tone is often the emotional center of a text and can reveal an author's attitude toward the theme.

HOW AUTHORS SET THE TONE

Authors use all kinds of tools to set the tone of a piece.

Figurative Language

Figurative language is language that means something different from its literal **INTERPRETATION**. Instead of writing something very plainly, an author might choose more imaginative words to express the same thing with tone.

> **INTERPRETATION**
> a way of understanding or explaining something

EXAMPLE:

He looked like he'd just stepped off a long-delayed flight from the end of the world.

Instead of just writing "He was tired," this sentence includes other images to add to the tone—the exhaustion and frustration of being on a plane for a long time, and the stress a person might feel if the flight was delayed and came from a far-away place.

Some types of figurative language are:

FIGURE OF SPEECH	PERSONIFICATION
IRONY	PUN
METAPHOR	SIMILE
ALLUSION	
(BIBLICAL, LITERARY, AND MYTHICAL)	

Connotative Language

CONNOTATIVE LANGUAGE goes beyond a word's simple meaning to the things that the word is associated with. An author might choose certain words to make use of its connotations to emphasize the tone.

EXAMPLE:

The pretty petals spread like lace over the ground.

If we say something is pretty, we mean it's pleasing to look at. But "pretty" also connotes that something is delicate and possibly feminine. So we wouldn't usually use it to write about a car.

A word doesn't just contribute its simple meaning to tone. It brings all its connotations with it as well.

Word Choice

Word choice refers to the decisions an author uses about what words to use.

EXAMPLE:

Say an author wants to describe a strong character but doesn't want to use the word "strong."

 If the author chooses "tough," the character might seem hard to approach.

 If the author chooses "steady," the character might seem boring.

 If the author chooses "powerful," the character might seem like a leader.

Slight variations between different words can add up to big differences in tone.

Rhyme and Repetition

Rhymes occur when the sounds at the end of words are the same. Repetition just refers to anything that happens again and again. Both rhyme and repetition can make language more intense or make it seem more playful, depending on how they're used.

EXAMPLE:

"It's almost time to turn the test in," Jim told Becky.

"I know," Becky said.

This exchange is pretty simple: Jim tells Becky something, and Becky tells him she already knows. However, if repetition is included, the tone shifts.

EXAMPLE:

"It's almost time to turn the test in," Jim told Becky.

"I know, I know, I know," Becky said.

Now Becky sounds pretty annoyed . . . almost as if Jim tells her stuff she already knows *all the time*. What if we add an exclamation point to the repetition?

EXAMPLE:

"It's almost time to turn the test in," Jim told Becky.

"I know! I know! I know!" Becky said.

This time Becky sounds pretty frantic, as if she's trying to wrap up the test before the end and is perhaps worried. Jim might just be trying to give her a hand because he can see she's working down to the wire.

ALLITERATION is a special kind of repetition, where the first letters of several words are all the same, such as: An Amazing Association of Alligators!

The tone can change through the repetition of the words and punctuation, but what happens if we use rhyme?

EXAMPLE:

"It's almost time to turn the test in," Jim told Becky.

"I know," Becky said. "And so, it's time to go!"

Suddenly, the tone has turned playful. The rhymes let us know that Becky thinks things aren't that serious at this point . . . and they might even signal that we're in the middle of a poem, where the regular rules of daily life don't always hold.

Similes and Metaphors

SIMILES and **METAPHORS** compare one thing to another. They are like a two-for-one deal in setting tone. Not only do they give the flavor of the thing that's described, but they also bring in all the feelings associated with the thing it's compared to.

> **SIMILE**
> a comparison of one thing with another

> **METAPHOR**
> a figure of speech in which a word or phrase is applied to an object or action where it does not literally apply

Simile:

Our friendship is like a tree with deep roots.

Don't forget that similes use the words "like" or "as" to make a comparison. Metaphors don't.

Metaphor:

Our friendship is a tree with deep roots.

These sentences express that a long friendship has some of the qualities of a tree with deep roots: It's sturdy and hard to dislodge, even in tough times.

Allusions

An ALLUSION is a reference to another work of art or culture. Allusions bring up our memories and associations with what they allude to, and the other work lends its tone to the new work. By making an allusion, an author is encouraging the reader to recall the other work's mood.

This is like the way a DJ may take a popular song and sample parts of it to make a new song—when you hear the new song, you remember the feelings you had for the old song, too.

EXAMPLE:

He's got a grin like the Cheshire Cat.

The Cheshire Cat is a character in ALICE'S ADVENTURES IN WONDERLAND. His grin is so powerful that it sticks around even after the cat's whole body vanishes! So when people say he's got a grin like the Cheshire Cat, they mean it's a memorable grin—and also perhaps a little bit fantastical, frustrating, or mysterious, because the Cheshire Cat in the fantasy frustrates Alice and remains a mystery.

Here's a visual summary of all the tools an author can use to create tone:

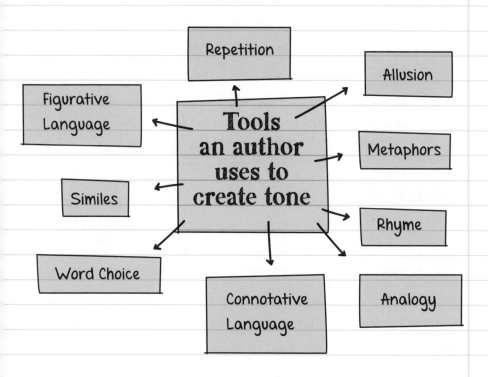

1. What figures of speech compare one thing to another?

2. What figure of speech compares something to another work of art or culture?

3. Define "rhyme."

4. Can you change the tone of a situation just by repeating a word?

5. Does connotative language depend only on the simple meaning of words?

6. What do we call the decisions a writer makes in selecting words?

7. True or false: Alliteration contributes to tone by making us think of all the other things the words used might mean.

8. Can the tone of a statement affect what it means, even if none of the words change?

9. Read this passage from VANITY FAIR, by William Makepeace Thackery. What is the tone of the passage? What words or devices give it that tone?

> About this time there drove up to an exceedingly snug and well-appointed house in Park Lane, a travelling chariot with a lozenge on the panels, a discontented female in a green veil and crimped curls on the rumble, and a large and confidential man on the box. It was the equipage of our friend Miss Crawley, returning from Hants.

10. Read this passage from A DOUBLE STORY, by George MacDonald. What is the tone of the passage? What words or phrases give it that tone?

> There was a certain country where things used to go rather oddly. For instance, you could never tell whether it was going to rain or hail, or whether or not the milk was going to turn sour. It was impossible to say whether the next baby would be a boy, or a girl, or even, after he was a week old, whether he would wake sweet-tempered or cross.

CHECK YOUR ANSWERS

1. Analogies, similes, and metaphors
2. Allusion
3. When sounds at the ends of words match
4. Yes
5. No
6. Word choice
7. False
8. Yes
9. The tone is conversational, confidential, gossipy, and opinionated. The author offers lots of opinions in the descriptions, like "exceedingly snug and well-appointed," and describes the characters as if describing them to a friend. The word "our" also makes readers feel as if they're part of a conversation with the author.

10. The tone is playful or fun. The author uses informal language like "you could never tell," which makes the reader feel like something unpredictable may happen. MacDonald uses lots of examples to give a sense of many possibilities.

#9 and #10 have more than one correct answer.

Chapter 22

POETRY

WHAT IS POETRY?

Poetry doesn't have a strict definition, but poets often use language in unusual ways to write about highly imaginative and emotional subjects.

"And, as imagination bodies forth
The forms of things unknown, the poet's pen
Turns them to shapes, and gives to airy nothing
A local habitation and a name."
— William Shakespeare,
A Midsummer Night's Dream

COMMON KINDS of POETRY
Narrative Poems

Just like stories and genres, a poem can fit into more than one category!

NARRATIVE POEMS tell a story—so to write one, a poet must have a story to tell.

EXAMPLE:

CASEY AT THE BAT, by Ernest L. Thayer, tells the story of a dramatic baseball game that begins like this:

The outlook wasn't brilliant for the Mudville nine that day;
The score stood four to two with but one inning more to play.
And then when Cooney died at first and Barrows did the same,
A sickly silence fell upon the patrons of the game.

A straggling few got up to go in deep despair. The rest
Clung to the hope which springs eternal in the human breast;
They thought if only Casey could but get a whack at that—
We'd put up even money now with Casey at the bat.

Lyrical Poems

LYRICAL POEMS are like songs in rhythm or subject matter. The lines rhyme and lilt very much like the lyrics of a song. Like songs, lyrical forms are more freewheeling than regular speech in some ways. In other ways they're more formal—like the fact that they must conform to a rhyme. So lyrical form allows for an unusually large range of meaning, but that meaning must be delivered in a specific form.

EXAMPLE:

An excerpt from "ODE TO H.H. THE NIZAM OF HYDERABAD," by Sarojini Naidu:

Sweet, sumptuous fables of Baghdad
The splendours of your court recall,   ← "Recall" and "festival" rhyme.
The torches of a Thousand Nights
Blaze through a single festival;
And Saki-singers down the streets,
Pour for us, in a stream divine,
From goblets of your love-ghazals
The rapture of your Sufi wine.   ← "Divine" and "wine" rhyme.

Free Verse

FREE VERSE poems do not follow any strict rhythm or meter. Free verse allows for just about any meaning, because there are no rules determining what these poems must be about— or how they should be said.

EXAMPLE:

An excerpt from "A FARM PICTURE," by Walt Whitman:

Through the ample open door of the peaceful country barn,
A sunlit pasture field with cattle and horses feeding,
And haze and vista, and the far horizon fading away.

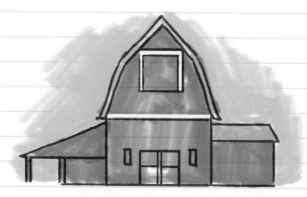

There is no rhyme, fixed structure, or set topic—
Walt Whitman wrote about what he wanted freely.

Ode

An ODE is a lyric poem that is written to a particular subject. An ode must be written _to_ something, so it will always be about a certain subject, and always addressed to that subject—and it could be any subject!

EXAMPLE:

DON'T FORGET THAT A STANZA IS A GROUP OF LINES THAT COMPOSE A SEGMENT OF A POEM.

The final stanza of John Keats's "ODE ON A GRECIAN URN" is written about a beautiful piece of ancient sculpture.

O Attic shape! Fair attitude! with brede
    Of marble men and maidens overwrought,
With forest branches and the trodden weed;
    Thou, silent form, dost tease us out of thought
As doth eternity: Cold Pastoral!
    When old age shall this generation waste,
      Thou shalt remain, in midst of other woe
Than ours, a friend to man, to whom thou say'st,
    "Beauty is truth, truth beauty—that is all
      Ye know on earth, and all ye need to know."

Ballad

A BALLAD is a poem that tells a story in short stanzas, often for singing. Since ballads tell a story, the poet needs a story to tell. Some ballads also have repeated lines, like songs do. When lines repeat, their meaning often changes—or grows more intense.

EXAMPLE:

An excerpt from "THE BALLAD OF JOHN SILVER," by John Masefield:

We were schooner-rigged and rakish, With a long and lissome hull,
And we flew the pretty colours of the crossbones and the skull;
We'd a big black Jolly Roger flapping grimly at the fore,
And we sailed the Spanish Water in the happy days of yore.

Epic

An EPIC is a long poem about a significant event, usually focused on a hero. To be an epic, a poem must tell a story, and that story must be about something significant, told through the adventures of some kind of hero.

EXAMPLE:

In the EPIC OF GILGAMESH, translated by William Muss-Arnolt, an arrogant king is confronted by a wild man conjured by a goddess.

> The **EPIC OF GILGAMESH** is one of the oldest stories in literature. It was written about 4,000 years ago!

And as the cattle were frightened, so were the people.
Like the doves, the maidens sigh and mourn.
The gods of Uruk, the strong-walled,
Assume the shape of flies and buzz about the streets.
The protecting deities of Uruk, the strong-walled,
take on the shape of mice and hurry into their holes.
Three years the enemy besieged the city of Uruk;
the city's gates were barred, the bolts were shot.
And even Ishtar, the goddess, could not make head
against the enemy.

Sonnets

A SONNET is a 14-line poem with 10 syllables of IAMBIC PENTAMETER per line. The form of a sonnet is so demanding that the poet may need to compromise meaning in some places to fit the form—or the demands of the form may force poets to discover new meanings they hadn't dreamed of before!

WHAT IS IAMBIC PENTAMETER?

An **IAMB** is a group of two syllables, with the emphasis on the second syllable. Like: "I am," or "da DUM," like a heartbeat. Pentameter is from the Greek root **PENT**, which means five. So five iambs is ten syllables with a particular emphasis and rhythm, like the following examples from William Shakespeare's "Sonnet 12":

When I do count the clock that tells the time
(which is read rhythmically like "When I / do count / the clock / that tells / the time")

This very famous line from Shakespeare's HAMLET is also iambic pentameter but with a slight twist:

"To be or not to be, that is the question."

If you read it closely, you can see this quote is actually 11 syllables. That's because sometimes poets add a "grace note" to the beginning of a line of iambic pentameter—a quick syllable that leads into the rest of the line.

EXAMPLE:

"HOW DO I LOVE THEE?" by Elizabeth Barrett Browning.

How do I love thee? Let me count the ways.
I love thee to the depth and breadth and height
My soul can reach, when feeling out of sight
For the ends of being and ideal grace.
I love thee to the level of every day's
Most quiet need, by sun and candle-light.
I love thee freely, as men strive for right.
I love thee purely, as they turn from praise.
I love thee with the passion put to use
In my old griefs, and with my childhood's faith.
I love thee with a love I seemed to lose
With my lost saints. I love thee with the breath,
Smiles, tears, of all my life; and, if God choose,
I shall but love thee better after death.

ANALYZING POETRY

Poetry doesn't always come right out and say what it means. Its FORM—the way poetry is written and the figurative language that is often used in poetry—affects its *meaning*. One way to think of poetry is as a puzzle to solve—look for the clues in a poem to figure out what the author is trying to convey.

Just as we analyze other types of fiction, we can analyze poetry—we can find explicit and implicit evidence in the poem. We can draw inferences from the writer's word choice and the form (how the writer breaks up stanzas, if the writer repeats lines, how the title figures into the poem, etc.).

EXAMPLE:

In the poem below, Christina Rosetti describes the happiness of being in love.

A Birthday
by Christina Rosetti

C.R. compares her heart to things that are natural and beautiful.

My heart is like a singing bird

C.R. thinks of her heart as beautiful and valuable, and feels that it is protected and provided for by her love.

Whose nest is in a water'd shoot;

C.R. compares her heart to places with plenty of food and water. These places are also safe and peaceful.

My heart is like an apple-tree

Whose boughs are bent with thickset fruit;

My heart is like a rainbow shell

That paddles in a halcyon sea;

This stanza is about how happy she feels.

My heart is gladder than all these

Because my love is come to me.

She is happy because her love has come to her.

Raise me a dais of silk and down;

Hang it with vair and purple dyes;

These lines sound like preparation for royalty or a grand celebration.

Carve it in doves and pomegranates,

And peacocks with a hundred eyes;

Work it in gold and silver grapes,

In leaves and silver fleurs-de-lys;

Because the birthday of my life

These lines mix language about French royalty and images that could be religious.

Is come, my love is come to me.

This is part of the title of the poem! It must be important. But why? Birthdays are the beginning of a new life. She is saying that her love makes her feel like she's just been born into a new life! The whole poem is about celebrating this feeling.

After **READING** and **ANALYZING** "A Birthday" line by line, we could argue that this is a *lyrical* poem about how love can be a new beginning.

We would use explicit evidence, like the word "birthday," to support that idea. One could also argue that the poem is about how love makes your life full and meaningful.

We could use the phrase "My heart is like an apple-tree / Whose boughs are bent with thickset fruit" as implicit evidence. We can infer from this simile that the person feels full of happiness.

Unlike most puzzles, there's no one "right" answer to what a poem means. The author usually does have a point he or she is trying to get across, but a lot of a poem is also open to interpretation—people who read it may understand it differently. And that's part of the fun of poetry—hearing what other people saw that you didn't and sharing the things you saw in a poem that somebody else didn't!

1. What two kinds of poems are most like songs?

2. What is the name for a group of lines in a poem?

3. What kind of poem has 14 lines of iambic pentameter?

4. How many syllables are there in a line of iambic pentameter?

5. True or false: A poem can't be an ode unless it is written to a specific subject.

6. True or false: A narrative poem does not tell a story.

7. True or false: An epic poem usually contains a hero.

8. True or false: The form of a poem can affect its meaning.

9. Read the following poem. What type of poem is it? How does the form affect word choice?

"Fire and Ice," by Robert Frost

Some say the world will end in fire,
Some say in ice.
From what I've tasted of desire
I hold with those who favor fire.
But if it had to perish twice,
I think I know enough of hate
To say that for destruction ice
Is also great
And would suffice.

10. Read the following poem and analyze it line by line:

"Success," by Emily Dickinson

Success is counted sweetest
By those who ne'er succeed.
To comprehend a nectar
Requires sorest need.

Not one of all the purple host
Who took the flag to-day
Can tell the definition,
So clear, of victory,

As he, defeated, dying,
On whose forbidden ear
The distant strains of triumph
Break, agonized and clear!

CHECK YOUR ANSWERS

1. Lyrical and ballad

2. Stanza

3. Sonnet

4. 10

5. True

6. False

7. True

8. True

9. "Fire and Ice" is a lyrical poem that focuses on feelings, so Frost must choose words that a person can experience. The form of the poem affects the meaning because the ideas must be conveyed simply, like in song lyrics, and the ideas must be conveyed in rhyme, which means that Frost has a smaller number of words he can choose from to explain his ideas.

10.

"Success," by Emily Dickinson   *Topic of the poem*

Success is counted sweetest ← *Success is sweet, like candy!*

By those who ne'er succeed.

To comprehend a nectar

Requires sorest need. ← *People who never succeed think success is the best thing that can happen.*

Not one of all the purple host

Who took the flag to-day ← *Perhaps refers to people who won at a game*

Can tell the definition,

So clear, of victory, ← *The winners can't describe success very clearly.*

As he, defeated, dying, ← *The people who win can't describe success nearly as well as people who want to win.*

On whose forbidden ear

The distant strains of triumph ← *The people who don't win understand success better because they want to win so badly!*

Break, agonized and clear!

#9 and #10 have more than one correct answer.

FICTION
READING LIST

"Fiction is like a spider's web, attached ever so lightly perhaps, but still attached to life at all four corners. Often the attachment is scarcely perceptible."
—Virginia Woolf, A ROOM OF ONE'S OWN

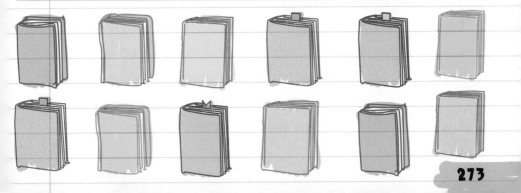

6th Grade FICTION Reading List

→ Adventure Comedy
→ Hole-arious!
→ A crazy juvenile detention camp makes
   kids go into the desert to dig holes all day
   to teach them a lesson . . . seems useless,
   but one of them realizes that they're really
   digging for treasure!

HOLES
Louis Sachar

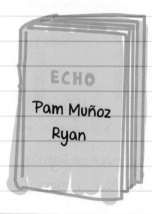

→ Multilayered Drama
→ Powerful
→ Five stories that link characters
   across two continents and show
   how music can overcome great
   fear and prejudice

ECHO
Pam Muñoz Ryan

→ Funny Fantasy
→ Head-buttingly awesome
→ A witch-in-training has to protect her
   home from the monsters of Fairyland with
   nothing but a frying pan and the help of a
   zany bunch of six-inch-tall blue wild men.

THE WEE FREE MEN
Terry Pratchett

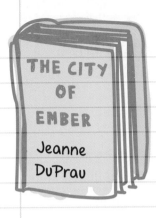

THE CITY OF EMBER

Jeanne DuPrau

→ Science Fiction
→ Underground mystery
→ The underground city of Ember is the last home of all humans . . . but it's slowly running out of power. Lina hears a secret. The secret might save everyone. Or it might ruin everything.

OUT OF MY MIND

Sharon M. Draper

→ Novel
→ Questions the norm
→ Molly cannot walk or talk, but she's determined to break through everyone's ideas of her and define herself.

WONDER

R. J. Palacio

→ Contemporary Fiction
→ Wonderful
→ The story of Auggie, an extraordinary kid who teaches his class how to "choose kind"

7th Grade FICTION Reading List

OKAY FOR NOW
Gary D. Schmidt

→ Historical
→ Drama
→ Doug Swieteck is a skinny punk whom other kids stay away from, but there's more to him than that. Set in the 1960s and guaranteed to make you cry like a baby.

AMERICAN BORN CHINESE
Gene Luen Yang

→ Graphic novel
→ Action-packed fable with a surprise twist
→ Three stories that answer: What happens when you're the only Chinese American student at your new school? Who is the Monkey King? And how do you ruin your cousin's life?

ENDER'S GAME
Orson Scott Card

→ Science Fiction
→ Great game
→ Ender is chosen by the military to fly to a space station to practice battle simulations against an invading force of bug-like aliens. But Battle School is hard enough to survive on its own.

THE WITCH OF BLACKBIRD POND
Elizabeth George Speare

→ American History
→ Suspensful
→ In colonial Connecticut, 16-year-old Kit is lonely . . . and her only friend, Hannah, is suspected of being a witch.

A SINGLE SHARD
Linda Sue Park

→ World History
→ Cuts deep
→ An orphan in 12th-century Korea works for a strict but brilliant pottery master who is seeking a Royal Commission. A sad and subtle journey.

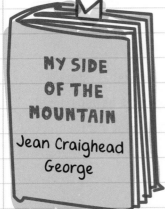

MY SIDE OF THE MOUNTAIN
Jean Craighead George

→ Nature Adventure
→ Survival
→ Sam runs away from home and sets up in a hollow tree in the Catskill Mountains. Now he just has to survive.

8th Grade FICTION Reading List

→ Science Fiction
→ Future tense
→ The main kid is the genetic clone of a drug lord, lives in a compound where everybody hates him, and he has no idea why he was made.

THE HOUSE OF THE SCORPION
Nancy Farmer

→ Fantasy
→ Heart theft
→ THIS BOOK IS THE BEST. READ IT NOW. A thief is hired by a magus to steal a jewel. The thief is clever. The magus is murderous. The story is unforgettable.

THE THIEF
Megan Whalen Turner

→ Sports
→ Sizzling
→ Lyrical all-star basketball story told in poetry about a baller named Filthy McNasty. Read it out loud.

THE CROSSOVER
Kwame Alexander

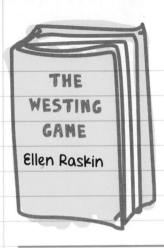

→ Mystery
→ Often imitated, never replicated
→ What is the best mystery you ever read? Did you say THE WESTING GAME? If not, then you have not read the best mystery ever. Fact.

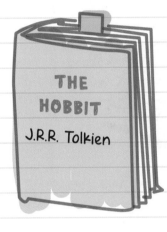

→ Fantasy
→ As good as the movies are bad
→ Bilbo is a comfort-loving homebody until a wizard shows up at his door and whisks him off on an adventure full of hungry trolls, murky forests, magic rings, and dragon's gold.

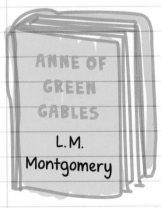

→ History
→ Delightful
→ A story about a girl who is vibrant and eager and talks too much. This book will charm anybody who reads it. A big, long series to dive into.

Unit 4

READING NONFICTION

Everyone loves a good story. But what if you're interested in THE FACTS? What if you want to learn something that you're sure is true in the world around you, not just in a writer's imagination? That's when you look for nonfiction. NONFICTION is **PROSE** writing based on fact. That doesn't mean you won't find stories in nonfiction—after all, the real world is full of stories. It's just that in nonfiction, the stories you read—whether they're journalism, essays, speeches, memoir, or more—are true!

> **PROSE**
> any writing that's not
> poetry or drama

Chapter 23

TYPES OF NONFICTION

Just like fiction, nonfiction comes in different *genres*, or types. If you're reading a news article, for instance, you don't expect the author to share her opinions on the events she's reporting or to tell her own personal story and discuss how it relates to the news. But if you pick up a personal memoir, you do expect the author to share his personal story. If you listen to a speech, you're probably hoping to hear the author's opinions.

Just like with genres in fiction, every nonfiction genre has its own <u>special features</u> and its own way of telling a true story.

TYPES and STRUCTURE of NONFICTION

Common types of nonfiction are:

LONGER-LENGTH NONFICTION

Literary Nonfiction uses the tools of literature to describe events in the real world.

Biographies are accounts of a person's life.

BLAH BLAH BLAH

THE STORY OF A KING

Memoirs are a person's own memories.

SHORTER-LENGTH NONFICTION

Journalism is writing intended to be published or broadcast by the news media, such as in magazines or newspapers, or on media websites and television.

Opinion Pieces share a person's opinion about a topic.

Expositions explain something.

Arguments state and defend a point of view.

Essays are short pieces of writing on a subject.

Personal Essays have a loose structure and come from a personal point of view.

Speeches are written and then spoken to an audience.

Epistles, or letters, are written to a person and published later— either as a collection of letters or as a single letter.

> Sometimes this category overlaps with poetry or other literary works. For example, Frankenstein was an EPISTOLARY NOVEL, which is a novel written in the form of letters.

COULD-BE-ANY-LENGTH NONFICTION

Historical Accounts describe history.

Scientific Accounts describe scientific discoveries or experiments.

Technical Accounts describe technical matters.

Economic Accounts describe events having to do with the economy.

JOURNALISM

Journalism aims to tell "the truth, the whole truth, and nothing but the truth." It's not a place where journalists share their own opinions or reveal details about their own lives. Instead, journalists REPORT on stories, which means that they do lots of research, making sure that every detail in their story is true and that every quote is recorded just as it was originally said.

Journalism also tends to be very <u>matter-of-fact</u> in the way it's written. Journalists don't usually use the tools of literature to create drama or tension, or save the most interesting parts for the end. Instead, their goal is to get the facts to the reader as quickly as possible. So in journalism, the most important facts go first and the less important ones follow.

LITERARY NONFICTION

Some of the best stories in life are true. Sometimes the dry delivery of journalism just won't do. A writer may want to tell a true story in a dramatic fashion, complete with plot tension, setting, character description, and dialogue. That's when he or she turns to literary nonfiction. It uses all the tools that a fiction author would use to tell an imagined story. The only difference? In literary nonfiction, the story's *true*.

BIOGRAPHY and MEMOIR

Biography and memoir are true stories that are personal and highlight an individual person's life. They might use the forms of literary nonfiction, including tools like plotting and dialogue. Or they might be more journalistic and just convey the facts. Chances are, they fall somewhere between the two.

> The author of the biography isn't usually involved in the story, but sometimes people do write their own **AUTOBIOGRAPHIES**.

> **AUTOBIOGRAPHY**
> a person's telling of his or her own life

Biography

Biography tells the story of a life or a part of a life. It's supposed to be **FACTUAL**, or rooted in the facts, and supported by research. A biographer might be able to interview the subject of a biography. Sometimes, though, the subject won't want to talk with the biographer or the biographer will be working after the subject has passed away. In those cases the biographer uses

letters, interviews, published reports, and anything else she can find to create a complete picture of the subject.

Memoir

A memoir is a piece in which the author writes down his or her own memories. Unlike biography, it doesn't have to be rooted in fact or research, although some memoirists do a lot of fact-finding and probing. The important thing for an author writing a memoir is not to get the history right, but to share his or her memories and perspective on them.

WHAT'S the DIFFERENCE?

Your choice of genres may be very different depending on **WHO** you're writing for and the point you want to make. Different genres alter the focus of the topic, so authors usually choose their genre carefully and for a purpose. A writer who wants to get the facts across quickly will probably work in a journalistic style. A writer who is interested in building tension and writing dialogue in a true story might choose to work with literary nonfiction. A writer who is mostly interested in recording his memories would be better off working

in memoir than doing all the research necessary to write an autobiography.

Depending on the genre of nonfiction, the same account can sound very different. For example, there are many different ways to write the following situation: The twins next door get their first remote-control model plane, and it somehow winds up on the neighbor's roof.

Journalism:

A remote-control model plane was found on the roof of the Millers' home in Roosevelt Circle on Tuesday afternoon. Twins Jeffrey and Jessica Jones admitted to owning the plane, but claimed they had no knowledge of how it had arrived there.

CHARACTERISTICS:

* Puts the most important facts first
* Reports only what sources have said
* Leaves out any opinions or personal history of the author

Literary Nonfiction:

A plane soared out of a vast and empty blue sky. For a breathtaking moment, it appeared to be on track to make a perfect landing on the lawn at the twins' feet. But then it made a strange, lurching turn and came to a rest two stories over their heads, on the roof of the home of the Millers, their next-door neighbors.

CHARACTERISTICS:

* Uses **PACING** to build tension
* Uses literary descriptive techniques
* Treats the subjects as characters

PACING
the speed at which things happen, change, or develop in a text

Biography:

One of the formative moments of Jessica's young life was the day that her model plane, on its inaugural flight, landed on the roof of her neighbors' home. In later years, both Jessica and Jeffrey claimed that they had been the remote pilot of the errant plane. But nobody was ever sure why both were so eager to take responsibility for the crash-landing—or which one of them had actually had their hands on the controls.

CHARACTERISTICS:

* Refers to research and other sources
* Focuses on the whole life of one individual
* Uses a blend of journalistic and narrative style

Memoir:

I knew that plane was flying too fast and too high.
But Jeffrey wouldn't listen to me. Just like me, he'd never
piloted a remote-control plane before. I think he just got
carried away, because a minute later, it had plunged out
of the sky and landed on the Millers' roof. I guess I can
tell the truth now, decades later. But Mom had already
been threatening to send Jeffrey to boarding school if
he got in any more trouble. I didn't know what I'd do
without him. So I said I did it. He took responsibility, too:
He tried to tell Mom that he was the one who did it.
But I was so good at sticking to my lines, even back
then, that Mom couldn't tell which one of us was telling
the truth. So she grounded us both. But she didn't send
him away. I think that's probably when I first knew I
might have a future as an actress.

CHARACTERISTICS:

* Focuses on the memories of an individual
* Doesn't refer to other research
* Personal, somewhat literary style

The EXPERIENCE?

As with fiction genres, the very same piece of nonfiction can become different depending on how we experience it. No matter what a text says, it makes a big difference how you experience it.

COMPARING STRUCTURES: NONFICTION VS. FICTION

Fiction and nonfiction can be about the same topics, but there are big differences in how the authors treat the topic.

> ## Reminder:
> These are the different ways you can experience nonfiction text:
>
> **AUDIO:**
> radio programs or audiobooks
>
> **VISUAL:**
> a regular ol' book, e-books, or comic books
>
> **LIVE:**
> a speech
>
> **MULTIMEDIA:**
> a documentary

EXAMPLE:

These excerpts are both about children who had to work in England in the 1800s. This passage from AN INDUSTRIAL HISTORY OF ENGLAND, by Henry de B. Gibbins, is an example of nonfiction:

SOMETIMES regular traffickers would take the place of the manufacturer, and transfer a number of children to a factory district, and there keep them, generally in some dark cellar, till they could hand them over to a mill owner in want of hands, who would come and examine their height, strength, and bodily capacities, exactly as did the slave owners in the American markets. After that the children were simply at the mercy of their owners, nominally as apprentices, but in reality as mere slaves, who got no wages, and whom it was not worth while even to feed and clothe properly, because they were so cheap and their places could be so easily supplied. Children were often worked 16 hours a day, by day and by night.

The following passage from OLIVER TWIST, by Charles Dickens, is an example of fiction:

THE ROOM in which the boys were fed was a large stone hall, with a copper at one end; out of which the master, dressed in an apron for the purpose, and assisted by one or two women, ladled the gruel at meal times. Of this festive composition each boy had one porringer, and no more—except on occasions of great public rejoicing, when he had two ounces and a quarter of bread besides. The bowls never wanted washing. The boys polished them with their spoons till they shone again; and when they had performed this operation (which never took very long, the spoons being nearly as long as the bowls) they would sit staring at the copper, with such eager eyes, as if they could have devoured the very bricks of which it was composed;

employing themselves, meanwhile, in sucking their fingers most assiduously, with the view of catching up any stray splashes of gruel that might have been cast thereon. Boys have generally excellent appetites. Oliver Twist and his companions suffered the tortures of slow starvation for three months; at last they got so voracious and wild with hunger, that one boy, who was tall for his age, and hadn't been used to that sort of thing (for his father had kept a small cook-shop), hinted darkly to his companions, that unless he had another basin of gruel *per diem*, he was afraid he might some night happen to eat the boy who slept next to him, who happened to be a weakly youth of tender age. He had a wild, hungry eye; and they implicitly believed him. A council was held; lots were cast who should walk up to the master after supper that evening, and ask for more; and it fell to Oliver Twist.

The evening arrived; the boys took their places. The master, in his cook's uniform, stationed himself at the copper; his pauper assistants ranged themselves behind him; the gruel was served out; and a long grace was said over the short commons. The gruel disappeared; the boys whispered to each other, and winked at Oliver; while his next neighbors nudged him. Child as he was, he was desperate with hunger, and reckless with misery. He rose from the table; and advancing to the master, basin and spoon in hand, said, somewhat alarmed at his own temerity:

"Please, sir, I want some more."

There are some similarities between the nonfiction and fiction account of child labor:

 Both writers discuss the lack of food.

 Both writers describe the cruel realities of being a poor child in England in the 1800s.

 The reader can infer from both texts that both writers were against child labor and could be writing to advocate for better care for children.

However, there are also <u>major differences</u> due to the genre:

NONFICTION: AN INDUSTRIAL HISTORY OF ENGLAND	FICTION: OLIVER TWIST
Focuses on all children who work in England	Focuses on one particular child
Doesn't have much descriptive detail	Describes how lots of things look and feel
Not set in any one place	Set in a specific place
No dialogue	Includes dialogue
Includes facts	Tells a story (no facts)

Why would an author choose to write fiction instead of nonfiction?

Nonfiction vs. Fiction

NONFICTION	FICTION
Nonfiction authors can use research—like old newspaper articles, interviews, eyewitness accounts, etc.	Fiction writers often use research, but fiction also offers the author a chance to use his/her imagination.
Nonfiction writers rely on verifiable facts.	Fiction writers do not rely on verifiable facts.
Nonfiction writers can include what a person is thinking and feeling by conducting interviews or verifying accounts.	The author creates what his/her characters are thinking and feeling, which is generally not as emphasized in nonfiction.
Nonfiction authors may find that the story that interests them most is a true one!	Fiction might give the author a chance to tell the story in the most dramatic way and stir the hearts and minds of readers.
Nonfiction often includes charts, graphs, captions, photos, illustrations, etc.	Fiction often includes illustrations or art.

NONFICTION VS. FICTION

CHECK YOUR KNOWLEDGE

1. Is nonfiction written about imaginary events?

2. What kind of nonfiction is published by the news media?

3. How can fiction and nonfiction treat the same topics in different ways?

4. What kind of nonfiction describes a person's own memories?

5. What kind of nonfiction defends a point of view?

6. Would an economic account be primarily about advances in satellite technology?

7. What kind of nonfiction explains something?

8. Would a historical account be primarily about historical events?

9. Read the following passage from WALDEN, by Henry David Thoreau. Is it a biography, a memoir, or an opinion piece?

At the approach of spring the red squirrels got under my house, two at a time, directly under my feet as I sat reading or writing, and kept up the queerest chuckling and chirruping and vocal pirouetting and gurgling sounds that ever were heard; and when I stamped they only chirruped the louder, as if past all fear and respect in their mad pranks, defying humanity to stop them. No, you don't—chickaree—chickaree. They were wholly deaf to my arguments, or failed to perceive their force, and fell into a strain of invective that was irresistible.

CHECK YOUR ANSWERS

1. No

2. Journalism

3. A fiction author can use his or her imagination to describe the thoughts, feelings, and motivations that drove real events, or fill in facts that can never be known. A nonfiction author writing about the same events has to stick to the facts.

4. Memoir or autobiography

5. Argument

6. No

7. Exposition

8. Yes

9. Memoir

Chapter 24

TEXTUAL ANALYSIS and EVIDENCE

Many of the tools that we use to read fiction can also be used to read nonfiction.

OBJECTIVE SUMMARY

An objective summary gives a brief explanation of something without adding our own personal opinions or judgments. In fact, an objective summary might be even more important in nonfiction than in fiction, because nonfiction is meant to highlight reality and facts.

FINS can help you swim through a piece of writing and write an objective summary:

Fact-check
Important facts only
No opinions
Sequence your facts

EXAMPLE:

THE STORY OF MY LIFE, by Helen Keller, describes how Helen would wander her family property as a little girl.

Even in the days before my teacher came, I used to feel along the square stiff boxwood hedges, and, guided by the sense of smell, would find the first violets and lilies. There, too, after a fit of temper, I went to find comfort and to hide my hot face in the cool leaves and grass. What joy it was to lose myself in that garden of flowers, to wander happily from spot to spot, until, coming suddenly upon a beautiful vine, I recognized it by its leaves and blossoms, and knew it was the vine which covered the tumble-down summer-house at the farther end of the garden! Here, also, were trailing

Opinion!

clematis, drooping jessamine, and some rare sweet flowers called butterfly lilies, because their fragile petals resemble butterflies' wings. But the roses—they were loveliest of all. *Opinion!* Never have I found in the greenhouses of the North such *Opinion!* heart-satisfying roses as the climbing roses of my southern home. They used to hang in long festoons from our porch, filling the whole air with their fragrance, untainted by any earthy smell; and in the early morning, washed in the dew, they felt so soft, so pure, I could not help wondering if they did not resemble the asphodels of God's garden. *Opinion!*

Just because a piece is nonfiction does not mean that no opinions are included—Helen Keller's account is full of her opinions. When we paraphrase, it's okay to state her opinions, as long as we say they are from her—after all, it is a fact that Helen Keller loved the roses of her home more than any others she found. We just need to avoid adding ~~our~~ own opinions when we're writing an objective summary.

EXAMPLE:

PERSONAL OPINION DOESN'T BELONG IN AN OBJECTIVE SUMMARY.

A paraphrase that is NOT objective:

Helen Keller loved the roses of her childhood home more than any others she ever found, but I think that's because she didn't experience all the best gardens of the world.

WHO CONCLUDED THIS? HELEN KELLER OR THE WRITER? IT'S UNCLEAR?

EXAMPLE:

A paraphrase that IS objective:

Helen Keller used to walk the grounds of her family home. She describes how she loved the roses there more than any others she ever found.

ATTRIBUTES THE SOURCE OF THE OPINION

EVIDENCE in a NONFICTION TEXT

Explicit evidence is evidence that comes right out and says something. Implicit evidence is evidence that is not clearly stated—but we can use it to draw conclusions or INFERENCES. The explicit and implicit evidence categories from fiction also apply to nonfiction.

EXPLICIT EVIDENCE EXAMPLE:

Someone in a news article is quoted as saying "I don't like dogs!"

This person explicitly says he or she does NOT like dogs—so we can claim this!

306

IMPLICIT EVIDENCE EXAMPLE:

Someone writes in an essay that they have always avoided heights.

We can **INFER** that this person probably has a fear of heights and does not want a career as a mountain climber.

> **DENOTATIVE**
> to be a sign or symbol of something

EXPLICIT VS. IMPLICIT TEXTUAL EVIDENCE

EXPLICIT EVIDENCE	IMPLICIT EVIDENCE
* Proof plainly stated in the text	* Proof only implied by what is stated in the text
* Inference can be made	* Inference can be made
* **DENOTATIVE**	* Connotative
* EXAMPLE: You know your friend spent the afternoon painting because you sat with her and watched while she painted.	* EXAMPLE: You know your friend spent the afternoon painting because you saw paint on her hands and clothes when you met up in the evening.
INFERENCE: Your friend spent the afternoon painting.	INFERENCE: Your friend probably spent the afternoon painting.

EVIDENCE in a NONFICTION TEXT

In SAILING ALONE AROUND THE WORLD, the author, Joshua Slocum, meets a fellow captain named Pedro Samblich.

Samblich was greatly interested in my voyage, and after giving me the tacks he put on board bags of biscuits and a large quantity of smoked venison. He declared that my bread, which was ordinary sea-biscuits and easily broken, was not nutritious as his, which was so hard that I could break it only with a stout blow from a maul. Then he gave me, from his own sloop, a compass which was certainly better than mine, and offered to unbend her mainsail for me if I would accept it. Last of all, this large-hearted man brought out a bottle of Fuegian gold-dust from a place where it had been cached and begged me to help myself from it, for use farther along on the voyage.

Nautical jargon that means removing a sail from its pole.

EXPLICIT EVIDENCE:
What Does the Text Clearly State?

1. Samblich gave Slocum tacks, biscuits, and venison.
2. Samblich thought his bread was more nutritious than Slocum's.
3. Samblich gave Slocum a compass.
4. Slocum thought Samblich's compass was better than his.
5. Samblich offered to help remove Slocum's mainsail.
6. Samblich offered Slocum gold dust.

IMPLICIT EVIDENCE:
What Conclusions Can We Draw from the Text?

EVIDENCE	IMPLICATION
Samblich gave Slocum many things.	Samblich was generous.
Samblich thinks his bread and his compass are better.	Samblich thinks he knows more than Slocum.
Slocum calls Samblich large-hearted.	Slocum is grateful to Samblich.
Slocum says his bread is easy to break, and Samblich's is hard.	Slocum disagrees that Samblich's bread is better.

The BEST EVIDENCE

Most nonfiction texts are full of evidence. But what if we only want to prove that Samblich is generous? Choosing the BEST evidence from all the evidence is crucial. We want to choose the details that will get the point across quickly and convincingly.

EXAMPLE:

Here's all the evidence about gifts being given in the passage:

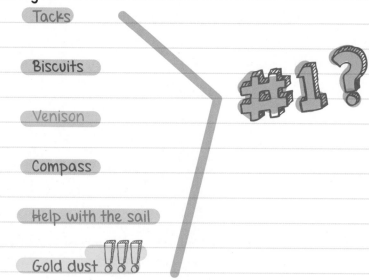

Samblich gives or offers Slocum:

Tacks

Biscuits

Venison

Compass

Help with the sail

Gold dust !!!

If we can only choose ONE piece of evidence, which piece of evidence makes Samblich seem most generous? What you choose as the best evidence is up for debate! Gold dust is way more precious than hard biscuits, so we might choose the gold dust—however, a compass could be even more useful for a sailor than gold dust. But maybe we find out that the author loves meat and was very hungry—then venison would be a really generous gift. Any of those choices might work, but it's unlikely that tacks or biscuits would be the best choice in this case.

1. A huge sign outside a clothing store says "SALE." You deduce that all the shoes inside are on sale. Do you know this from explicit or implicit evidence?

2. True or false: You can search for evidence in a nonfiction text, but not in fiction, because it's imaginary.

3. True or false: Implicit evidence is evidence that is stated clearly in the text.

4. Define "inference."

5. True or false: Both nonfiction and fiction contain explicit and implicit evidence.

6. True or false: An objective summary should not contain anyone's opinions.

7. True or false: An objective summary should not contain the opinions of the writer of the summary.

8. Read this passage from THE PERSONAL RECOLLECTIONS OF ST. JOAN OF ARC, by Mark Twain:

> I was sent to Domremy, to the priest, whose housekeeper became a loving mother to me. The priest, in the course of time, taught me to read and write, and he and I were the only persons in the village who possessed this learning.

What explicit evidence shows that the priest and Joan of Arc were better educated than the rest of the village? What implicit evidence shows that the priest thought it was important for Joan of Arc to learn to read and write?

9. True or false: You can use implicit evidence to draw an inference.

10. Your friend says it's fine if you come over, but you can tell from her voice that she's too tired to have much fun, so you decide to see her later. Did you use explicit or implicit evidence?

ANSWERS ➤

CHECK YOUR ANSWERS

1. Explicit

2. False

3. False

4. A conclusion that we come to using evidence and reason

5. True

6. False

7. True

8. Explicit evidence: The priest and Joan of Arc are the only two in the town who know how to read and write.

Implicit evidence: The priest spends the time to teach Joan of Arc how to read and write; therefore, he must think it is important.

9. True

10. Implicit

Chapter 25

AUTHORSHIP

WHO WROTE THIS?

We tend to think of authors as the people who write novels and poems. But in fact, anyone who writes anything is an author, whether they're writing fiction, like poetry, or nonfiction, such as science textbooks.

In memoirs, autobiographies, and journalistic pieces, "I" refers to the author's own POINT OF VIEW (POV).

These are some factors that impact an author's POV:

What time in history was this author writing?

What is the author trying to convince you of as the reader?

What events in their upbringing and personal life influenced their writing style and the evidence they chose to include?

An author always has a unique perspective and purpose—it's your job to figure out what it is.

AUTHOR BACKGROUND and PERSPECTIVE

Just like in fiction, an author's biographical background can affect the way he or she writes nonfiction. An author's biographical background (his or her life story, culture, historical time, location, experiences, etc.) affects his or her perspective and writing—even when writing about facts.

EXAMPLE:

Compare these two passages about riverboats, one by Maxim Gorky, who was born in Russia in 1868, and one by Mark Twain, who was born in America in 1835.

From THROUGH RUSSIA, by Maxim Gorky (published in 1923):

> The water of the river was smooth, and dull silver of tint. Also, so barely perceptible was the current that it seemed to be almost stagnant under the mist of the noontide heat, and only by the changes in the aspect of the banks could one realize how quietly and evenly the river was carrying on its surface the old yellow-hulled steamer with the white-rimmed funnel, and also the clumsy barge which was being towed in her wake.

Dreamily did the floats of the paddle-wheels slap the water. Under the planks of the deck the engines toiled without ceasing. Steam hissed and panted. At intervals the engine-room bell jarred upon the car. At intervals, also, the tiller-chains slid to and fro with a dull, rattling sound. Yet, owing to the somnolent stillness settled upon the river, these sounds escaped, failed to catch one's attention.

From Mark Twain's speech on Fulton Day at Jamestown, 1907:

You probably do not know a great deal about that boat. It was the most important steamboat in the world. I was there and saw it. Admiral Harrington was there at the time. It need not surprise you, for he is not as old as he looks. That little boat was interesting in every way. The size of it . . . You see, the first and most important detail is the length, then the breadth, and then the depth . . . Then her tonnage—you know nothing about a boat until you know two more things: her speed and her tonnage. We know the speed she made. She made four miles—and sometimes five miles. Now comes the tonnage of that boat. Tonnage of a boat means the amount of displacement; displacement means the amount of water a vessel can shove in a day.

Both writers are writing about steamboats, but they're writing from opposite sides of the world. Their perspectives create different texts.

GORKY

Focuses on the river around the boat

Describes his sensory experiences

Doesn't find the boat very interesting

TWAIN

Focuses on the boat

Describes the dimensions and technical abilities of the boat

Says it's the most important boat in the world

Were the steamboats Gorky and Twain describing really that different? Probably not. Gorky and Twain were different, so they saw the boats differently.

Gorky had just lived through a very difficult time in Russian history, with a great deal of conflict, war, and change. It makes sense that he would focus on his surroundings, because understanding the big picture would have been important in a time of conflict. Or, one could argue that he focused on nature because it was the only constant in a time of great change.

But Twain was writing during a time in American history when new technology was introducing big changes to the world. It makes sense that he would focus on the technological details of the boat, because at the time the whole country was interested in new technology and everything it seemed to promise for the future.

WHAT'S the AUTHOR'S PURPOSE?

Every author writes with a **PURPOSE** in mind: the reason an author sat down to write in the first place. To understand a piece of writing, we must think about the author's purpose.

In some nonfiction writing, like opinion pieces, it is an established fact

> When analyzing an author's purpose, ask, "Does the author want P.I.E.?" Does the author want to PERSUADE, INFORM, or ENTERTAIN?

that the authors have a purpose and are trying to convince the reader of something.

DON'T VOTE FOR JOE JEROME
BY ALLAN ALLANDALE, *mayoral candidate*

My Brother Should Not Be Mayor
by Suzie Jerome

The first headline announces DON'T VOTE FOR JOE JEROME. However, the **BYLINE** says it was written by Joe Jerome's opponent. The second headline states MY BROTHER SHOULD NOT BE MAYOR. However, the byline says Joe Jerome's sister, Suzie Jerome, wrote it. In both these cases, the biography of the writer affects how he or she wrote the article and how you read the article.

> **BYLINE**
> tells you who is the author of an article

It would be easy to see that Joe Jerome's opponent isn't just trying to inform you of the issues. He wants to win. That affects his perspective and the way he tells the story. He's more likely to highlight bad things about Joe and leave out Joe's good qualities.

On the other hand, you might assume that Joe Jerome's sister would be on his side. She could have a lot of reasons for not wanting him to be mayor.

> Maybe she knows he's ill, and she's trying to protect his health.

> Maybe she's jealous and doesn't want to see him succeed.

> Or maybe she simply thinks he would be a terrible mayor!

The reader would have to remember that his or her point of view is also a personal perspective and may have more to do with personal opinions than with politics.

Besides persuasive writing, most types of nonfiction writing are meant to be written as objectively as possible. Still, the author's perspective and purpose affect what he or she writes. For example, scientific papers are only meant to share the results of scientific research. However, perhaps someone has attacked the scientist's ideas, and the scientist must defend his or her ideas. Or, what if the scientist did a study on something small but believes his or her findings should be applied to a broader field? These realities, and many more, can affect the way the "facts" are written.

Finding the Author's Purpose

How do we figure out an author's purpose? Sometimes they'll come right out and tell us:

EXAMPLE:

> The purpose of this paper is to show that the calculations that Doctor Zhivago published last year were incomplete.

However, most writers don't come right out and say what they mean. We can figure it out for ourselves by looking at the details that a writer chooses to concentrate on and the details he or she chooses to omit. For example, if a scientific article does nothing but attack the ideas of another scientist, we can deduce that the author wants everyone to know the other scientist was wrong. We can also deduce by the author's lack of new discoveries that perhaps the author hasn't had any recent breakthroughs in his or her own lab.

EXAMPLE:

Patrick Henry made the following speech on March 23, 1775, at St John's Church in Richmond, Virginia, shortly before the American Revolution began:

Gentlemen may cry, Peace, Peace—but there is no peace. The war is actually begun! The next gale that sweeps from the north will bring to our ears the clash of resounding arms! Our brethren are already in the field! Why stand we here idle? What is it that gentlemen wish? What would they have? Is life so dear, or peace so sweet, as to be purchased at the price of chains and slavery? Forbid it, Almighty God! I know not what course others may take; but as for me, give me liberty or give me death!

Henry doesn't come right out and say "The purpose of this speech is to encourage Americans to start a revolution." However, look at the facts he chooses to highlight:

- Others are already fighting.
- We are standing idle.
- The war is on its way to us.

All of the evidence he points to suggests that the American people should fight.

Also, look at the questions he asks:

- Why are we idle?
- Is peace worth it if we don't have freedom?

All of the questions he asks suggest that the American people should fight.

We get the best sense of what Henry means in his famous last line:

"I know not what course others may take; but as for me, give me liberty or give me death!"

Henry begins by saying he doesn't know what others might do, but by the time he finishes, it's pretty clear he thinks everyone should fight for freedom, just like he says he will.

CONFLICTING EVIDENCE and VIEWPOINTS

Whenever anyone has an idea, there's probably another person who has a conflicting one. The same can be said for evidence.

A good writer knows that not everybody agrees—even when the facts seem irrefutable. So, the author will mention

> **CONFLICTING VIEWPOINT EXAMPLE:**
> That cat is lazy. **vs.** That cat is tired.
>
> **CONFLICTING EVIDENCE EXAMPLE:**
> I saw the cat climb down the wall. **vs.** I saw the cat fall off the wall.

those other points of view and pieces of evidence in his writing—and explain why they shouldn't count. This is called a COUNTERCLAIM or **COUNTERARGUMENT**. Acknowledging other points of view (especially opposing points of view) makes one's argument stronger because it shows forethought. Plus, it gives the writer a chance to refute those points and show

> **COUNTERARGUMENT**
> reasons used to oppose an idea or argument

why his or her opponent's argument is not so sturdy.

EXAMPLE:

In this selection from "Eugenics and Other Evils,"
G. K. Chesterton explains his arguments, his opponents'
arguments, and why he is correct.

PINK = CHESTERTON'S OPINION
BLUE = OPPONENTS' OPINIONS (AS TOLD BY CHESTERTON)

There exists to-day a scheme of action. It is a thing that can
be pointed out; it is a thing that can be discussed; and it is a
thing that can still be destroyed. It is called for convenience
"Eugenics"; and that it ought to be destroyed I propose to prove
in the pages that follow. I know that it means very different
things to different people; but that is only because evil always
takes advantage of ambiguity. I know it is praised with high
professions of idealism and benevolence; with silver-tongued
rhetoric about purer motherhood and a happier posterity. But
that is only because evil is always flattered, as the Furies were
called "The Gracious Ones." I know that it numbers many
disciples whose intentions are entirely innocent and humane;
and who would be sincerely astonished at my describing it as
I do. But that is only because evil always wins through the
strength of its splendid dupes; and there has in all ages been a
disastrous alliance between abnormal innocence and abnormal
sin. Eugenics itself, in large quantities or small, coming quickly
or coming slowly, urged from good motives or bad, applied to a
thousand people or applied to three, Eugenics itself is a thing no
more to be bargained about than poisoning.

CHESTERTON'S VIEWPOINT	OPPOSING VIEWPOINT	CHESTERTON'S ARGUMENT
Eugenics is a distinct movement.	Eugenics means different things to different people.	Evil is always vague.
Eugenics is evil.	Eugenics is about idealism, motherhood, and posterity.	Evil is often disguised as good.
It doesn't matter if the people who believe in eugenics are good or bad.	People who believe in eugenics have good intentions.	Eugenics is evil either way.

Good writers don't just express their side of the argument.

Like Chesterton, they anticipate what the other side might have to say. Then they gather evidence to refute the claims of the naysayers and strengthen their own arguments.

COMPARE and CONTRAST DIFFERENT PRESENTATIONS

Even when nonfiction is written about actual historical events, authors can present events very differently. A personal essay won't read the same as a journalistic article. A speech won't be written the same as a dictionary entry—even if all of them are about the exact same thing.

Speech EXAMPLE:

I'd like to thank my mother, who instilled in me a love of all flowers, but especially daffodils, from a very young age. In fact, I just discovered the most beautiful hill of daffodils I've ever seen while on a walk in the woods today. There must have been thousands of them there, and as a member of this horticultural society, I couldn't resist strolling down the hill. When I got to the bottom, I found a patch unlike anything I'd ever seen, orange and yellow and white. Of course, as a good horticulturalist, I had to collect a sample. I'd like to present them this evening to my mother, without whom none of my achievements in the horticultural world would have been possible.

Characteristics:

* The author's tone is geared to an audience of more than one. (It's obvious that the author is speaking to a group.)

* The author's tone is conversational. (It's not too formal or dry.)

* The author speaks from his or her personal point of view. (The author describes personal experiences and how they've shaped his or her perspective.)

News Article EXAMPLE:

Daffodil scientists reported an as-yet-unsolved break-in today at a major daffodil research facility hidden deep in the woods outside Detroit. Vandals apparently scaled a six-foot fence to destroy a large swath of the  precious experimental blossoms. Officials were particularly baffled by the theft of a stand of experimental orange blossoms, known at the facility for their terrible smell.

Characteristics:

* The author's tone is more matter-of-fact. (It is not conversational.)

* The author focuses on the immediate reporting of the facts. (There isn't much background information or follow-up on what happened next.)

* The author writes only verifiable facts and is sure to mention when something is not confirmed by using words like "apparently."

Biography EXAMPLE:

No one ever discovers who broke in or why!

The unsolved break-in at the McMurdo Daffodil Research Facility proved to be a pivotal moment in the history of daffodil research and the life of Ceslaw Finbromovich, its primary champion. After the daffodils were destroyed, security at the site was called into question, and many major donors declined to continue funding. Heartbroken, Finbromovich changed his name and joined the circus, where he catapulted to international fame as Finn Flowers. But his lifelong dream to discover whether daffodils might actually be the long-sought cure for insomnia was lost forever.

Characteristics:

* The author focuses on conveying facts—some of which may have only been released long after the incident. (Nobody else identified the actual name of the site.)

* The author focuses on the long-term reporting of the facts. (There is background information and follow-up on what happened next.)

* The author uses literary techniques to tell the story, structuring a plot, explaining characters' motivations, and building drama with phrases like "lost forever."

1. True or false: An author's biography affects his or her fiction writing but not his or her nonfiction writing.

2. True or false: The place where an author grew up can affect the way she writes a scientific paper.

3. Explain what an author's purpose is.

4. True or false: The purpose of a piece of writing will never be different from what the author says it is.

5. Read the following passage from THROUGH THE MAGIC DOOR, by Sir Arthur Conan Doyle. What is the author's purpose?

> I care not how humble your bookshelf may be, nor how lowly the room which it adorns. Close the door of that room behind you, shut off with it all the cares of the outer world, plunge back into the soothing company of the great dead, and then you are through the magic portal into that fair land whither worry and vexation can follow you no more.

6. Read this passage from Mary Wollstonecraft's VINDICATION OF THE RIGHTS OF WOMEN. What is the author's viewpoint? What is the opposing viewpoint?

> The education of women has, of late, been more attended to than formerly; yet they are still reckoned a frivolous sex, and ridiculed or pitied by the writers who endeavor by satire or instruction to improve them.

7. True or false: When a good writer builds an argument, he won't mention the opinions of people who might disagree with him.

8. True or false: Someone who tells her own story will not always have the same perspective as her biographer.

9. True or false: A biographer will never contradict the opinions of the person he is writing about.

10. True or false: A journalist's culture might affect the way she writes about a story.

1. False

2. True

3. An author's purpose is the reason why he or she is writing something.

4. False

5. The author's purpose is to show that it doesn't matter where or what you read—reading can transport you to a new and better place.

6. The author believes that women are gaining more access to education. Yet, opponents believe that women are frivolous, and pity and ridicule them.

7. False

8. True

9. False

10. True

Chapter 26

CENTRAL IDEAS and ARGUMENTS

WHAT'S the BIG IDEA?

A CENTRAL IDEA is the most important idea in a piece of writing. It's the idea that was so interesting that it got the author to sit down and start writing. It's the thing the reader keeps reading to learn more about. It appears throughout a piece of writing, from the beginning to the end.

DEVELOPING a CENTRAL IDEA

The author conveys the central idea by choosing details that help the reader understand it better.

When an author presents details that explain the central idea, he or she is DEVELOPING the central idea. That just means offering the reader more facts or details that expand the central idea.

> Think about the central idea as an umbrella over the whole piece—everything important in the piece is covered by the central idea. Anything NOT about the central idea is repelled or rolls off.

EXAMPLE:

Monarch butterflies are travelers. Every fall, they migrate in big flocks from the Great Lakes region of the U.S. and Canada to the evergreen forests of Central Mexico. Along the way, they can fly as fast as 25 miles per hour and as high as 11,000 feet. The trip isn't a short one, either. By the time they reach Mexico, those big flocks of butterflies have traveled approximately 2,500 miles.

The central idea of this passage is that monarch butterflies are travelers. The writer develops it by including relevant details, like:

They migrate from the U.S. to Mexico.
They fly 25 miles per hour.
They fly up to 11,000 feet.
They fly 2,500 miles.

WHAT IS an ARGUMENT?

An argument is a piece of writing where the author tries to convince the reader to agree with his or her central idea. The author sticks with a central idea throughout the piece and includes reasons and evidence for believing in that idea.

EXAMPLE:

"You shouldn't borrow my shoes!" she told her sister.
"But I always let you borrow my things," she replied.
"Yeah, but there AREN'T EVEN any frogs in Spain!" she replied.

That argument doesn't make any sense! The girl is most likely wrong, for one thing—there are probably some frogs somewhere in Spain. But that doesn't matter, because the girl is breaking the first rule of having an argument: She's not sticking with her central idea. If you don't stick to the central idea, you can't argue successfully.

DEVELOPING an ARGUMENT

An argument is more than just a disagreement. In a disagreement, people can simply make claims or state that something is the case without any reason.

EXAMPLE:

"Well, the shoes are mine, too."

"No, they're not!"

"Yes, they are."

"No, they are not!"

Evidence and Reason

An argument goes beyond claims—in an argument, a claim is backed up with **REASON** and evidence (verifiable facts and details that support the claim).

> **REASON**
> reasonable logic that persuades others to agree with the idea

EXAMPLE:

"They're mine!"

Reason!

"No, they're not. I bought them, and I can show you the receipt.

Evidence!

SHOES-R-US
one pair of shoes
$5
$5

So, you can't simply state a claim and leave it at that. To fully develop an argument, you must offer your reason (or reasons) and information that supports your point.

EXAMPLE:

THE FUNDAMENTAL PRINCIPLE OF A REPUBLIC is a speech Anna Howard Shaw gave in New York City in 1915. Her claim was that women should have the right to vote. She reasoned that if women cannot vote, then the state of New York is NOT a republic. Her evidence was the definition of a republic.

"Now what is a republic? Take your dictionary, encyclopedia, lexicon, or anything else you like and look up the definition and you will find that a Republic is a form of government in which the laws are enacted by representatives elected by the people."

Shaw builds the foundation of her argument on evidence—the definition of a republic.

> "Now when did the people of New York ever elect their own representatives? Never in the world. The men of New York have, and I grant you that men are people, admirable people, as far as they go, but they only go half way."

She lays out her reasoning by noting that New York does not fit the definition of a republic because only men get to vote—and they are only half of the population.

> "There is still another half of the people who have not elected representatives, and you never read a definition of a Republic in which half of the people elect representatives to govern the whole of the people."

She returns to her evidence and reiterates her reasoning—New York does not meet the basic requirement for being a republic because not everyone can vote.

Without reasoning and evidence, Shaw's claim would not stand up on its own or win a debate. She also remains consistent throughout by tying everything back to her central idea—women should have the right to vote.

Evidence and reasoning play on ETHOS (credibility), PATHOS (emotion), and LOGOS (logic). You can argue in different ways for different reasons. For example, if you are trying to convince your parents of something versus trying to convince a lawmaker of something versus trying to convince your best friend of something . . . you would use different **TONES**, **WORD CHOICES**, **ANALOGIES**, and more . . .

By tweaking your argument to have the appropriate credible information, emotional impact, and logic, you can more effectively convince your reader.

Tone in Argument

The way an author writes about a subject and how he or she creates the mood of the piece can also affect whether or not a reader is persuaded. All of the tools that fiction and nonfiction writers use can help set a tone in an argument and win over the audience, too. Such as:

* WORD CHOICE—choosing just the right word to express your message exactly
* FIGURATIVE MEANING—using language that's not strictly literal
* CONNOTATIVE MEANING—thinking about how a word is usually used and how that affects what it means
* ANALOGIES—comparing two things that are alike
* ALLUSIONS—referring to other cultural works

WORD CHOICE

The words you choose can make your argument weaker or stronger.

EXAMPLE:

That book is good.

VS.

That book is fast-paced and full of fascinating descriptions so you can't stop reading.

Simply writing that something is "good" doesn't tell the reader much about it or why the writer thinks it is good (and why the reader of the argument should agree). However, in the second example, the author carefully chooses specific words that get to the heart of what is unique and why it matters:

"fast-paced"

"fascinating descriptions"

"can't stop reading"

Because of word choice, we know exactly what makes the book so good—and we are more persuaded to read it ourselves!

ANALOGIES

An analogy can help people imagine more clearly what you're saying.

EXAMPLE:

I don't think it's a good idea to take this step without more preparation.

VS.

Taking this step without more preparation is like jumping out of an airplane without a parachute.

Suddenly, the author has everyone's attention. Everyone knows just how bad an idea he or she thinks it is—and what the consequences might be.

EVALUATING ARGUMENTS

How do you know if an argument is good or not? Go back to the definition of an argument: reasoning and evidence. To have a strong argument that can withstand a debate, the reasoning and evidence must be strong, too.

Sound Reasoning

When reasoning is strong, we call it SOUND. Reasoning is sound if:

> All of its parts are true.

> It leads us to the conclusion we were aiming for.

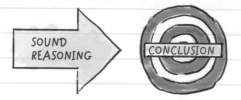

Unsound Reasoning EXAMPLE:

Some people report feeling cramps when they go swimming immediately after eating. So swimming must cause stomachaches.

In the example above, one thing does come after the next. But the reasoning isn't sound, because there isn't enough evidence to prove that swimming causes stomachaches. Lots of other things could cause them, like a fear of water or getting seasick.

Sound Reasoning EXAMPLE:

> If a person is planning to be in the sun, he or she should wear sunscreen. The sun emits powerful rays that can damage skin and ultimately cause cancer, even when it doesn't cause a visible burn. But multiple studies have proven that sunscreen protects skin both from burns and from sun damage that may be initially invisible.

The argument that people should wear sunscreen is supported by sound reasoning and evidence. The reasoning is sound because there is a strong relationship between not wearing sunscreen and sun damage, which is supported by scientific evidence.

Relevant and Irrelevant Evidence

Sound reasoning relies on strong evidence. Evidence is strong if it supports the argument and closely relates to the central idea of an argument—we call that **RELEVANT EVIDENCE. IRRELEVANT EVIDENCE** is information that is not connected to the central argument.

RELEVANT EVIDENCE
body of facts and information that support the central argument

IRRELEVANT EVIDENCE
body of facts and information that are not connected to the central argument

EXAMPLE:

If you are arguing that the price of blueberries is expensive compared to that of other fruit, the following is

SALE

BLUEBERRIES
$2.99/PINT
STRAWBERRIES
$1.99/PINT
CHERRIES
$4.99/POUND

RELEVANT EVIDENCE:

1. The price of blueberries

2. The price of strawberries
   (compared to the price of blueberries)

3. A conversion of the price of a pound of cherries into a pint of cherries so that the price can be compared to that of blueberries

IRRELEVANT EVIDENCE:

1. The way you feel about blueberries

2. The price of blueberry pies (not a fruit)

3. Any information about the time you won a blueberry pie eating contest

COMPARING AUTHORS and ARGUMENTS

The perspective of an author can change the way he or she writes a story—and the same is true for an argument. Depending on an author's background and purpose, he or she may:

> Use different reasoning to make the argument

> Emphasize different aspects of the argument

> Present different facts to support the argument

EXAMPLE:

These two authors have different perspectives and, thus, different arguments about whether the school should sell sugary drinks to students.

Say No to Sugary Drinks!

By Vanessa Victorinox

When we're thirsty, we shouldn't have to deal with additives like flavoring, caffeine, and sugar. We should be able to reach for the one thing we actually need: water. ←—VANESSA'S CENTRAL IDEA

347

SOUND →
EVIDENCE
We're all made up of water—about 60 percent of our body mass is water. Our bodies use water to carry nutrients to cells, so it's no wonder SOUND →
REASONING we get thirsty—that's an important job! Lakes and rivers aren't filled with soda, because soda MORE →
REASONING isn't a basic requirement for life. Water is. The National Center for Health Statistics reported that sugary drinks have been linked to "poor diet quality, weight gain, obesity, and, in adults, type 2 diabetes." So why would we put vending machines full of them in our schools? Let's stay healthy together—by drinking pure water.

MORE SOUND EVIDENCE

We Deserve a Choice!

OPPOSING
ARGUMENT

Sam Sweeting

SAME FACT USED IN VANESSA'S ARGUMENT,
BUT SAM USES THIS DETAIL TO OPPOSE VANESSA

We're all made up of a lot of water. But we're not *just* water. What makes us special is the parts of THIS IDEA
ISN'T
SUPPORTED
WITH FACTS. us that aren't just water—the special flavor that makes each one of us who we are. That's why I like soda from time to time. The bubbles and THIS ISN'T →
PARTICULARLY
RELEVANT. flavor make the day more interesting. Some of the drinks contain sugar, but some contain fruit juices or are fortified with vitamins. They provide SOUND
EVIDENCE calories, which everyone needs for energy.

Furthermore, it's important that I get to make my own choice, even about things like drinking water or soda. Making a good decision is part of growing up. If you never give me a choice to make, how can I learn how to make a good one?

↖ *SOUND REASONING*

SOUND ARGUMENT CHECKLIST:

✔ There is a claim.

✔ The claim is supported by evidence and reason.

✔ The tone is persuasive—consider word choice, figurative meaning, connotative meaning, analogies, and allusions.

✔ Everything relates to the central idea.

✔ All of the facts are true.

✔ The reasoning is sound.

✔ All of the evidence is relevant.

1. True or false: The central idea of an argument can't be found in the details.

2. True or false: A central idea only appears in one place in a text, not throughout the whole thing.

3. True or false: A claim is a statement that is not supported by reason or evidence.

4. True or false: An argument is a statement that is supported by reason or evidence.

5. Read this passage. Is it an example of sound reasoning? Why or why not?

> Upon investigating the scene, the detective found a book with the student's name written in it. Based on this discovery, he concluded that the student herself must have been at the scene.

6. Read this passage. Then write your own counterargument, using one of the facts that the author uses in the passage.

> Studies have shown that students learn more when their class sizes are smaller. The classic interpretation for this is that teachers are able to spend more time with each student and give each student more specialized instruction. But what about the things students learn from each other? Bigger class sizes aren't fashionable, but the more students in a class, the more perspectives each student can gain from. It's not just the teacher who does the teaching.

7. True or false: Two authors making arguments about the same topic must use all the same facts.

8. True or false: An author might choose to use particular words in order to set the tone of an argument.

9. True or false: Irrelevant evidence doesn't support the argument.

ANSWERS

CHECK YOUR ANSWERS

1. False

2. False

3. True

4. True

5. No. Someone else might have written the student's name in the book or taken the book to the scene.

6. Studies have shown that smaller class sizes benefit students. Some argue that a larger class size offers greater diversity of perspectives among the student body, but with too many students in class, not all of those perspectives will get heard. That's why studies suggest that learning decreases as class sizes grow. Students learn best from each other, and from a teacher, in smaller groups.

7. False

#6 has more than one correct answer.

8. True

9. True

Chapter 27

STRUCTURE

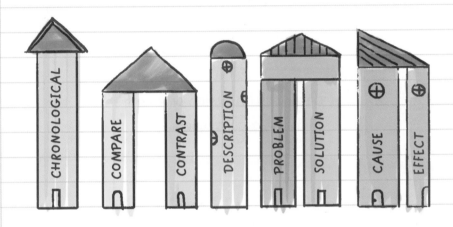

CHRONOLOGICAL · COMPARE · CONTRAST · DESCRIPTION · PROBLEM · SOLUTION · CAUSE · EFFECT

STRUCTURE is the organization of a text—or how the pieces fit together. Some common structures in nonfiction are:

{
COMPARE AND CONTRAST STRUCTURE
analyzes what is similar
about two or more
things and also what is different.
}

353

CHRONOLOGICAL STRUCTURE

organizes events by
when they happened.

PROCESS STRUCTURE

explains the series of actions of
how they happen.

← This structure often overlaps with chronological and cause and effect structures.

CAUSE AND EFFECT STRUCTURE

describes an action or event
and its consequences.

PROBLEM AND SOLUTION STRUCTURE

explains a problem and
offers a solution.

DESCRIPTION STRUCTURE

gives an account of something
by offering the relevant details,
characteristics, and information.

A piece of writing can blend or combine structures as well.

One way to differentiate between the types of text is to look for these <u>signal words</u>:

Text Type	Purpose	Signal Words
COMPARE and CONTRAST	Shows how two or more things are similar and/or different	in comparison by contrast similarly but on the other hand on the contrary yet however despite as opposed to
CHRONOLOGICAL or PROCESS	Shows the order or ranking of a series of actions	first next then before after 1,2,3, . . . last finally A,B,C, . . .

Text Type	Purpose	Signal Words
CAUSE AND EFFECT or PROCESS	Shows the relationship between two or more events or experiences; shows why something happens or the chain reaction of what will happen next	for this reason thus since in order to as a result therefore consequently because due to on account of
PROBLEM and SOLUTION	Outlines and highlights a dilemma and ways to solve it or address it	problem solution because research develop cause since as a result in order to so that goal investigate

Text Type	Purpose	Signal Words
DESCRIPTION	Shows an account of something by offering characteristics of the topic	No signal words— instead look for lots of descriptive details

Major Sections

The major sections of a piece of writing are the big pieces that make up the whole.

In a **NEWS ARTICLE**, the major sections are:

HEADLINE: the big title that appears above the article

LEAD (or LEDE): the first lines of the article, which contain the main idea

BODY: contains the elaboration and details of the main idea

Generally, news articles are structured like this:

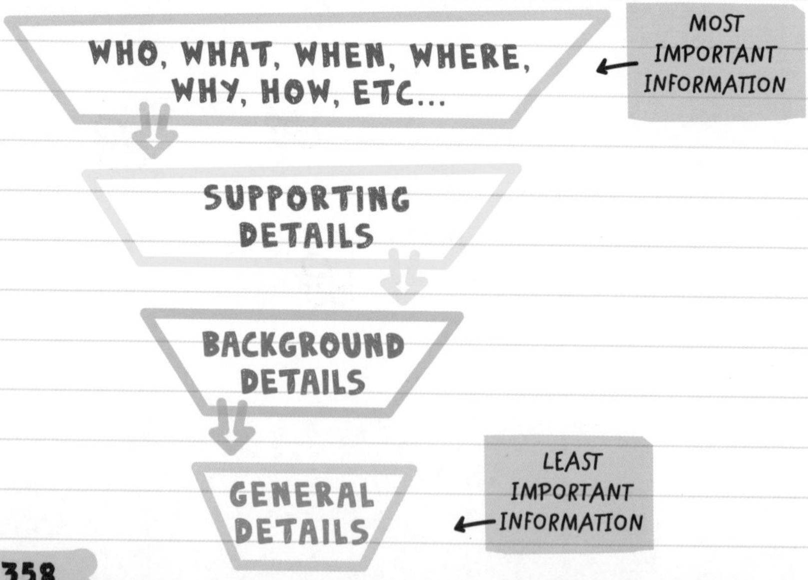

WHO, WHAT, WHEN, WHERE, WHY, HOW, ETC... ← MOST IMPORTANT INFORMATION

SUPPORTING DETAILS

BACKGROUND DETAILS

GENERAL DETAILS ← LEAST IMPORTANT INFORMATION

In an **ARGUMENT**, the major sections are:

Some teachers call this **GROUNDS**.

INTRODUCTION OF THE ARGUMENT → MAIN POINT ONE

MAIN POINT TWO ← SUPPORTING EVIDENCE

Some teachers call this **WARRANTS**, or the explanation of the evidence that connects it to the grounds.

The number of main points can vary. → SUPPORTING EVIDENCE → CONCLUSION

In a **BIOGRAPHY**, the major sections often are:

INTRODUCTION OF THE PERSON → DESCRIPTION OF HIS/ HER EARLY LIFE

HIS/HER MOST IMPORTANT ACCOMPLISHMENTS/ MAJOR EVENTS IN LIFE

HIS/HER EFFECTS OR IMPACT ON SOCIETY AND HISTORY

359

How Each Part Contributes to Structure

Each style of nonfiction has its own structure with different main sections. But no matter what the sections are, all of them are necessary to form a complete piece.

EXAMPLE:

You pick up a newspaper, but it is missing the first page. On page two, you discover that a man was running down the street, barefoot and carrying half a pineapple. But without the beginning section, you have no idea how he got there or why.

The same thing is true with arguments. If someone tells you, "You should never eat chocolate ice cream!" you might be willing to listen to them. But if they haven't got any evidence to back their claim up, you're probably not going to be convinced. To make a good argument, you need all the parts: the claim AND the evidence AND reasoning to support it. Often the genre dictates the order of the structure.

This article appeared in THE AFRO-AMERICAN LEDGER on January 11, 1908.

BIRTHDAY CELEBRATED

The headline gets our attention.

Was Seventy-Five Years Young

The lead tells the reader the article's central idea.

Unionville, MD, Jan 11—The anniversary dinner of Mrs. Nannie Gibson, was held December 26, at the residence of her son Mr. J. T. Coffer. Those present were Rev. and Mrs. Dennis, Mr. and Mrs. Henry Green, Mr. and Mrs. Stephen Bouldin. All enjoyed the affair, but none more so than the "young" lady herself, who was 75 years old that day.

The body gives us all the details.

A news article has a strict structure. Similarly, chronologically structured pieces follow a timeline. An argumentative essay, however, can shift in time if it serves the argument. However, every part contributes to the structure—we won't know what the author is trying to prove if we don't read the introductory claim. On the flip side, if we don't read the conclusion, we may not know where the argument finally ends!

KEY INDIVIDUALS and EVENTS

A good author doesn't just throw everything on the page at once. An author uses structure to:

Introduce key individuals and events

Illustrate and elaborate on them

Make connections and **DISTINCTIONS** between individuals and events

DISTINCTION
something that is different

EXAMPLE:

In this passage from the autobiographical memoir THE ROAD, the author, Jack London, tells how he begged for food while crisscrossing the country as a hobo.

Elaborates distinction: The man doesn't stop eating in front of a hungry person.

Introduces the narrator: the author, a hobo who is hungry.

There was one house in particular where I was turned down that evening. The porch windows opened on the dining room, and through them I saw a man eating pie—a big meat pie. I stood in the open door, and while he talked with me, he went on eating. He was prosperous, and out of his prosperity had been bred resentment against his less fortunate brothers.

Introduces a key actor: a man. Also makes a distinction— the man is not a hobo— he lives in the house and is well fed.

Elaborates distinction again!

The evidence leads the author to draw a conclusion.

He cut short my request for something to eat, snapping out, "I don't believe you want to work." Now this was irrelevant. I hadn't said anything about work. The topic of conversation I had introduced was "food." In fact, I didn't want to work. I wanted to take the westbound overland that night.

"You wouldn't work if you had a chance," he bullied.

I glanced at his meek-faced wife, and knew that but for the presence of this Cerberus I'd have a whack at that meat pie myself. But Cerberus sopped himself in the pie, and I saw that I must placate him if I were to get a share of it. So I sighed to myself and accepted his work-morality.

"Of course I want work," I bluffed.

"Don't believe it," he snorted.

"Try me," I answered, warming to the bluff.

"All right," he said. "Come to the corner of blank and blank streets"—(I have forgotten the address)—"tomorrow morning. You know where that burned building is, and I'll put you to work tossing bricks."

"All right, sir; I'll be there."

He grunted and went on eating. I waited. After a couple of minutes he looked up with an I-thought-you-were-gone expression on his face, and demanded:

"Well?"

"I . . . I am waiting for something to eat," I said gently.

"I knew you wouldn't work!" he roared. . . .

"In the meantime—" I began; but he interrupted.

"If I gave you something to eat now, I'd never see you again. Oh, I know your kind. Look at me. I owe no man. I have never descended so low as to ask any one for food. I have always earned my food. The trouble with you is that you are idle and dissolute. I can see it in your face. I have worked and been honest. I have made myself what I am. And you can do the same, if you work and are honest."

"Like you?" I queried.

Alas, no ray of humor had ever penetrated the sombre worksodden soul of that man.

"Yes, like me," he answered.

"All of us?" I queried.

"Yes, all of you," he answered, conviction vibrating in his voice.

"But if we all became like you," I said, "allow me to point out that there'd be nobody to toss bricks for you."

Author uses dialogue to develop the individuals in the story and explain a key event—the author outwits the man.

364

The author
elaborates
on the wife.
The author
mentions a
flicker in
her eye and
distinguishes
her from her
husband again.

I swear there was a flicker of a smile in his wife's eye. As for him, he was aghast—but whether at the awful possibility of a reformed humanity that would not enable him to get anybody to toss bricks for him or at my impudence, I shall never know.

You can also think about structure as a way of finding out:

WHO AND WHAT IS IMPORTANT?
The author probably starts by introducing key individuals and events.

WHY ARE THESE PEOPLE OR THINGS IMPORTANT?
The author most likely will illustrate and elaborate on them.

Lastly, an author may use structure to show **WHY SOMEONE OR SOMETHING IS UNIQUE OR PART OF SOMETHING GREATER.** If that's the goal, the author will make connections and distinctions between individuals and events.

EXAMPLE:

Robert Stawell Bell introduces the famous astronomer Galileo in his book GREAT ASTRONOMERS: GALILEO GALILEI.

Galileo's father may turn out to be a key individual.

Author elaborates on family circumstances and how they affect Galileo.

This line is the logical conclusion of the fact before it: Galileo had musical talent, so he learned to play an instrument.

This new revelation about Galileo builds on the facts we already know about his artistic talents.

This profile of Galileo begins at Galileo's birth, so it's probably a chronological structure.

GALILEO WAS BORN at Pisa, on 18th February, 1564. He was the eldest son of Vincenzo de Bonajuti de Galilei, a Florentine noble. Notwithstanding his illustrious birth and descent, it would seem that the home in which the great philosopher's childhood was spent was an impoverished one. It was obvious at least that the young Galileo would have to be provided with some profession by which he might earn a livelihood. From his father he derived both by inheritance and by precept a keen taste for

Elaborates on Galileo and his father

music, and it appears that he became an excellent performer on the lute. He was also endowed with considerable artistic power, which he cultivated diligently. Indeed, it would seem that for some time the future astronomer entertained the idea of devoting himself to painting as a profession. His father, however, decided that he should study medicine. Accordingly, we find that when Galileo was 17 years of age, and had added a knowledge of Greek and Latin to his acquaintance with the fine arts, he was duly entered at the University of Pisa.

This sentence moves the reader to the next chronological step in Galileo's life. But it's also the logical conclusion of everything else we've learned previously.

Again, we are learning about the character of both Galileo and his father—his father is practical, and Galileo obeys him.

1. True or false: Not all the sections of a piece of writing are necessary to fully understand it.

2. What is the structure of a newspaper article?

3. List three common structures in nonfiction.

4. True or false: The structure of a piece of writing doesn't affect its meaning much.

5. What structure does the following passage use?

   Town officials have struggled for the past several years over the problem of what to do with the windfall of leaves and branches that litter city streets after big storms. But I propose a new solution: Rather than deal with the organic matter as waste, collect and chip it, and sell it to city residents to fund the installation of beautiful new lighting on our city streets.

6. True or false: When an author elaborates on an event, it is the first time the author mentions it.

7. True or false: An author would never use an analogy to make a connection between two characters.

8. Write a headline for this news item:

> Over a hundred students met in the streets of Mulberry this afternoon as part of a large volunteer effort to collect branches and leaves damaged in last night's storm from the trees that line the city's streets. Students arrived shortly after school ended, and by nightfall, around 9 p.m., they had filled the beds of half a dozen pickup trucks with sticks, leaves, and branches.

9. Does this paragraph belong in the introduction, body, or conclusion of a piece of writing?

> Finally, from all the evidence gathered here, we can see clearly that the plan to collect damaged limbs and fallen leaves from the streets of Mulberry was a resounding success. The streets are cleaner and also better lit—thanks to the new lights we were able to install with the proceeds of the sale of garden chips made from damaged tree limbs that would have otherwise been discarded.

10. True or false: When an author makes a distinction between two characters, the author is pointing out what they have in common.

ANSWERS ▸ 369

CHECK YOUR ANSWERS

1. False

2. Headline, lead/lede, body

3. Any three of the following: compare and contrast, chronological, cause and effect, problem and solution, description

4. False

5. Problem and solution

6. False

7. False

8. Mulberry Students Save City Streets

9. Conclusion

#8 has more than one correct answer.

10. False

NONFICTION
READING LIST

"Truth is always strange, stranger than fiction."
—Lord Byron, DON JUAN

6th Grade NONFICTION Reading List

TRACKING TRASH

Loree Griffin Burns

→ Environment
→ Horror story
→ A group of scientists track trash from city garbage cans all the way out into the ocean, where it collects into terrifying islands of junk.

BAD NEWS FOR OUTLAWS

Vaunda Micheaux Nelson

→ American History/Biography
→ Best western
→ The life story of Bass Reeves, a U.S. Marshal and former slave, who brought law to the Wild West

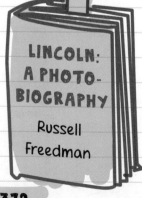

LINCOLN: A PHOTO-BIOGRAPHY

Russell Freedman

→ American History/Biography
→ Leadership training
→ Tons of pictures tell the story of a great president whose life was full of bravery and drama and whose death shocked the country.

→ Memoir/Free Verse
→ Heartbreak and joy
→ Gorgeous prose about what it was like to be an African American girl living in the shadow of Jim Crow and seeing the light of the Civil Rights movement

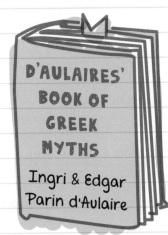

→ Mythology
→ Olympic achievement
→ All the great stories about Zeus and the Olympians, but with good writing this time

→ History
→ Fun with failure
→ Fourteen massive screwups by famous people will make anyone feel better about trying and failing, and trying again

7th Grade NONFICTION Reading List

AMELIA LOST
Candace Fleming

→ History
→ The ace
→ One of the most famous pilots in history, her mysterious disappearance, and the worldwide search for her and her missing aircraft

---

THE SURRENDER TREE
Margarita Engle

→ History/Free Verse
→ Fighting for freedom
→ Poems about Cuba in 1986, after three wars for independence, and still no freedom. Hard and beautiful to read.

BOMB
Steve Sheinkin

→ History/Science
→ A goodness explosion
→ A thriller set in World War II, where scientists race to invent the atomic bomb and spies race to sabotage it

→ Financial Literacy
→ Money talk
→ Forget a lemonade stand. Think lemonade brand, and learn how to earn, invest, and save.

HOW TO TURN $100 INTO $1,000,000
James McKenna and Jeannine Glista with Matt Fontaine

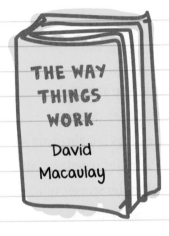

→ Science
→ Engineering marvel
→ How do can openers work? How do cranes work? How do pens work?

THE WAY THINGS WORK
David Macaulay

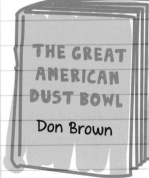

→ Comics/History
→ The gritty facts
→ A graphic novel about that one time America almost choked to death in one of the most destructive natural events ever

THE GREAT AMERICAN DUST BOWL
Don Brown

8th Grade NONFICTION Reading List

FRIDAY NIGHT LIGHTS

H.G. Bissinger

→ Sports
→ Can't lose
→ The greatest sports book ever written

RADIOACTIVE!

Winifred Conkling

→ History/Biography/Science
→ Something for everyone
→ Not one, but TWO thrilling stories about brilliant female scientists unlocking the secrets of nuclear fission and changing history

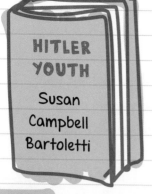

HITLER YOUTH

Susan Campbell Bartoletti

→ World History
→ Leave us kids alone!
→ Terrifying account of how Adolf Hitler formed the largest youth group in history and indoctrinated them to become his soldiers

→ Art/Design
→ Master class
→ This legendary graphic designer teaches a 101 course on typography, color theory, and everything else you need to have great taste.

→ Comics/Biography
→ Comics classic
→ A graphic novel about a survivor of the Holocaust, set in a world where the Nazis are cats and the Jews are mice

→ Memoir
→ Youngest recipient of the Nobel Peace Prize—EVER
→ Even a gunshot to the head can't keep this girl down. Malala speaks out about her journey and her fight for the right to an education.

WRITING

Everyone needs tools to write well—and not just pencil and paper. Understanding the basics of researching, writing, and editing, as well as knowing all the nitty-gritty details, like which connecting words help introduce ideas, all come together to create great writing. Some of the most common forms of writing are:

Arguments

Informative texts

Explanatory texts

Narratives

Once you know how to write these, you can write almost anything!

Chapter 28

RESEARCHING FOR WRITING

RESEARCH

RESEARCH is investigation to answer questions and discover new knowledge. We research to get new information and explore our own ideas further.

When we research, we first must look for **SOURCES**—anything or anyone that can give us information. You can get your information from lots of different **MEDIUMS**. ← A source can be another text, or it could be something not even written down—it just depends on what you need for your writing.

"MEDIA" OFTEN REFERS TO MASS COMMUNICATION, BUT "MEDIA" IS ALSO ANOTHER PLURAL FORM OF "MEDIUMS."

MEDIUM
a way in which information is delivered

Before you begin to research, you must have a clear idea of what issues you want to learn about and which questions you need to explore. You may want to start by creating a RESEARCH QUESTION, which is simply a question that maps out exactly what you want to research.

Good Research Question
EXAMPLE:

What laws have been proposed in the United States in the last ten years to close the wage gap between men and women?

This question <u>works well</u> because it is specific, so it offers a clear path for research.

Bad Research Question
EXAMPLE:

What laws are about wages?

This question <u>does not work well</u> because it is so broad that it will be difficult to research, and because it does not have a clear purpose or reason why someone might want to know the answer.

Good Research Question
EXAMPLE:

How does the author treat the subject of magic in THE ENCHANTED FAUN?

This <u>question works well</u> because it is focused enough to result in a clear answer, but broad enough for that answer to be complex and interesting.

Bad Research Question
EXAMPLE:

What happens at the end of THE ENCHANTED FAUN?

This question <u>does not work well</u> because the answer is too specific. It does not require much research beyond turning to the last page of the book, and it does not offer much opportunity for thought or discussion.

SOURCES

These sources can provide information for fiction writing or evidence to support arguments or analysis:

Literary sources

Fiction is imaginary, but that doesn't mean we can't learn anything from it. First of all, fiction is often carefully researched by the author, who might have learned a lot about the historical time or a certain place to write about it accurately and in great detail. But whether a fiction piece is heavily researched or not, it can often tell us something about the time in which it was written: how an author thought and felt about the world around him or her. Some literary sources are:

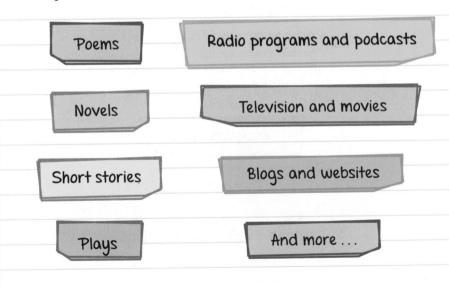

Poems

Radio programs and podcasts

Novels

Television and movies

Short stories

Blogs and websites

Plays

And more . . .

Nonfiction sources

No matter what kind of nonfiction, we know we're always going to find one thing in it: facts. Often that's what we're looking for when we do research. So nonfiction is frequently where we'll turn to find our information. Some nonfiction sources are:

Newspapers

Scientific papers

Magazines

Expert interviews

Radio programs and podcasts

Video presentations

Encyclopedias

Dictionaries

Reputable websites and blogs

And more . . .

Credibility of Sources

Not every source is **CREDIBLE**. If your
brother is always borrowing money
from you but never pays you back, then
he's not very credible when he says,
"I promise I'll pay you back this time!"

> **CREDIBLE**
> able to be believed

The strength of your argument
depends on the strength of the
supporting evidence. If a source isn't credible, the evidence
could be wrong, biased, or inaccurate, and thus your
argument would not hold up either.

How do you know if a source is credible? Ask the following
questions:

Does the author have a good reputation?
  * Do other writers trust his or her work?
  * Has the author been published in respectable
    publications?

Does the publisher have a good reputation?
  * Do other writers rely on this publisher for
    information?
  * Has the publisher published other works that
    people quote and use in their writing?

How recent is the information?
- ✴ Is the source from the correct time period?
- ✴ Is the information up-to-date?

Does the information match another reliable source?
- ✴ Do two or more other reliable sources show the same information?

Using Multiple Sources

Even when your source is credible, he or she probably doesn't know everything. To get the whole picture, use multiple sources.

EXAMPLE:

Two eyewitness accounts describe the sinking of the TITANIC in April 1912. Elizabeth Shutes, a governess on the ship, wrote:

Our lifeboat, with 36 in it, began lowering to the sea. This was done amid the greatest confusion. Rough seamen all giving different orders. No officer aboard. As only one side of the ropes worked, the lifeboat at one time was in such a position that it seemed we must capsize in mid-air. At last the ropes worked together, and we drew nearer and nearer the black, oily water. The first touch of our lifeboat on that black sea came to me as a last good-bye to life, and so we put off—a tiny boat on a great sea—rowed away from what had been a safe home for five days.

Washington Dodge, a doctor on the ship, wrote:

The officers in charge of loading the boats were cool and masterful, preventing as far as possible all disorder and enforcing the command to care for women and children first. When boat 13 was lowered to A deck to be loaded I went to this deck—After 8 or 10 women had been placed aboard, no further women or children were within hearing to respond to the officers' call. →

A number of men then climbed over the rail into the boat when someone pushed me from behind and shouted, "Get in doctor!" I climbed in and in a few moments the boat was filled and orders given to lower. As we were lowered, boat 15, which had been loaded from the boat deck, was also being lowered. By this we were for a few minutes placed in a perilous position, which threated our destruction. We observed as we neared the water that our boat was being lowered directly into the immense volume of water thrown out from the ship's side by the condenser pump. On the *Titanic* this was a stream about three feet in diameter, which was thrown with great force six or eight feet from the ship. It would instantly have swamped our boat. To add to our anxiety, boat 15 had swung directly over our heads, owing to the fact that the steamer had settled several feet into the water at her bow. Both boats were being lowered when our loud cries of warning were heard above and the lowering of both boats arrested. We had no officer or seaman in our boat to direct us, but fortunately were able to disengage an oar, and with it push the bow of our boat, which overhung the threatening waters from the pump, eight or ten feet from the ship's side, when releasing the trigger we dropped into the water and were at once swept away from the steamer's side by great force of the water.

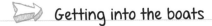

Both accounts share similar events and describe:

➭ Getting into the boats

➭ The lowering of the boats

➭ No officers in the lifeboats

➭ Trouble with lowering the boats

➭ Landing on the open sea as the TITANIC sank

However, there are also differences:

➭ Shutes describes confusion on deck, whereas Dodge describes order.

➭ Shutes gives a brief description of the nautical technology, and Dodge gives a detailed description of the nautical technology.

➭ Shutes doesn't describe much of what the people in her boat did, and Dodge explains that the residents of his boat shouted for help and used an oar to stay safe.

Neither Shutes nor Dodge is wrong; they just know different things. So to get the whole picture, you need to read both sources—and maybe some more!

PLAGIARISM and CITATION

When writing, it's important to avoid stealing someone else's ideas—that's **PLAGIARISM**! You must always give credit to the original author or publisher for their own work. Make sure you **CITE** the source or include a **CITATION** if:

> **PLAGIARISM**
> taking someone else's idea, phrasing, or data and passing it off as your own

> **CITE**
> referencing the source
>
> **CITATION**
> reference to the source

You use someone else's ideas.

← EVEN IF YOU PARAPHRASE THEM IN YOUR OWN WORDS!

You use someone's exact words.

When <u>not</u> to cite? If the information is common knowledge. Often during research, we paraphrase or restate ideas or information to include only the stuff we need from a source. Paraphrasing can help us avoid plagiarizing a source because we put the research in our own words. However, even if it's in

WORDS WORDS

390

our own words, it's still not our own idea, so we must cite the source! Any time you mention someone else's ideas or anything they've discovered in their original research—even if you paraphrase them—you have to cite them as the source.

How to Cite

There are several different styles of citation, and different teachers like different styles. However, most teachers ask for a page at the end of a report with citations of all the research resources used. Each citation will most likely include:

AUTHOR: the person who wrote it

LIKE AN ESSAY IN AN ANTHOLOGY

TITLE (and if it is part of a larger work, its title, too)

PUBLISHER: the company that printed and distributed the work

DATE OF PUBLICATION: for a book, just the year; for an article, date and the year

LOCATION OF PUBLICATION: usually just city and state

PAGE NUMBER: where the quote can be found in the piece

There are different style guides that explain how a citation should be formatted. The American Psychological Association (APA), the Modern Language Association (MLA), and the Chicago Manual of Style (CMS) produce some of the most popular style guides. Each teacher has his or her own favorite style, so remember to ask which to use for any writing assignments.

Generally used in social science publications, like research papers.

There are also websites that can help you create a citation—ask your teacher if he or she uses such a website and which ones are the best to use.

Book Citation EXAMPLES:

APA format:

Dumas, Alexandre. (1844). *The Three Musketeers*. Paris, France: Musketeer Publishing.

MLA format:

Dumas, Alexandre. *The Three Musketeers*. Paris: Musketeer Publishing, 1844. Print.

MLA citation includes the format of the information.

CMS format:

[1]Dumas, Alexandre. *The Three Musketeers*. Paris: Musketeer Publishing, 1844.

There will also be a small 1 in the body of your text where the material from this source appears.

While the information is mostly the same, keep a close eye on the differences in punctuation.

Website Citation EXAMPLES:

APA format:

Biblio, Mariana T. (2015, April 30). *The Joy of Books.*
Retrieved from http://www.worldsbestlibrary.com/joyofbooks

Instead of the website address, the MLA uses the title of the site.

MLA format:

Biblio, Mariana T. "The Joy of Books." *The World's Best Library.* American Librarian Publishers. 30 April 2015. Web. 15 May 2015.

Date the article was accessed by the researcher—NOT the date of publication

The MLA includes the publisher of the website when possible. If you don't know the publisher, just write N.P. for "No Publisher."

CMS format:

Biblio, Mariana T. "The Joy of Books." The World's Best Library. April 30, 2015. Accessed May 15, 2015. http://www.worldsbestlibrary.com/joyofbooks.

CITING SPECIFICS

When you use more than one research resource, you may need to cite where you got a specific piece of information in the body of your writing (next to the information or words you are citing). Again, a citation will look different according to the various styles.

APA format:

Sentence with information (Author, Year of Publication).

EXAMPLE:

D'Artagnan was one of the musketeers (Dumas, 1844).

MLA format:

Sentence with information (Author, Page Number).

EXAMPLE:

D'Artagnan was one of the musketeers (Dumas, 15).

CMS format:

Sentence with information.[1]

EXAMPLE:

D'Artagnan was one of the musketeers.[1]

This is a **FOOTNOTE**! It tells readers to look at the bottom of the page or the end of the document for a regular full citation.

When you cite a website for a specific detail, it'll look just the same as when you cite a book—except in MLA style, which uses page numbers. Because there are no page numbers on the web, just include the author's name so your readers can find the source on the citation page.

CITING QUOTATIONS

Sometimes you may want to include the exact words written or spoken by someone else—you can do so with quotations. Simply provide some context, use correct punctuation, and attribute its source (either in the context or as you would cite a specific detail). Again, ask your teacher what style to use when citing quotations.

Citation in Context EXAMPLE:

In *Narrative of the Life of Frederick Douglass*, Frederick Douglass disabuses Northerners who think slaves sing because they are happy, when he writes, "Slaves sing most when they are most unhappy. The songs of the slave represent the sorrows of his heart; and he is relieved by them, only as an aching heart is relieved by its tears."

Citing Specifics EXAMPLE:
(APA format)

Douglass disabuses Northerners who think slaves sing because they are happy, when he writes, "Slaves sing most when they are most unhappy. The songs of the slave represent the sorrows of his heart; and he is relieved by them, only as an aching heart is relieved by its tears" (Douglass, 1845).

FURTHER RESEARCH
and
REFOCUSING RESEARCH

Sometimes when you start trying to find out the answer to a question, you wind up with more questions.

EXAMPLE:

You have to write a report comparing two animals that are local wildlife. The frogs in the swamp behind your house make a racket after dark, so you go online to do some research. You discover these aren't just any frogs. The frogs behind your house are bullfrogs—the biggest kind of frog in North America. Not only that, but you read that you can tell a male from a female by the eardrums they have behind their eyes. In males, the eardrum is bigger than the eye; in females, it's about the same size. Also, the females themselves grow to be bigger than the males—sometimes a whole eight inches bigger!

That would raise some questions, wouldn't it?
Questions like:

Why do they make so much noise?

> Why do male bullfrogs have bigger eardrums
> than female bullfrogs?

> Why do female bullfrogs grow bigger
> than male bullfrogs?

Those would all be questions for further research.

However, your teacher wants you to compare two different local animals in your report. You might start off researching frog sounds, but then you must research the different sounds that other local animals make—cows, dogs, birds, etc. You discover that birds in different areas of the country actually have special accents—a bird hatched in Michigan sings differently than that same species hatched in Georgia. So then you begin researching more about your region's birds and their songs.

When we discover something in the course of our research that sends us down another appropriate path, that's called REFOCUSING research. It happens often and it's a sign that there's more to learn.

CHECK YOUR KNOWLEDGE

1. True or False: It's not plagiarism if you use someone else's ideas but not their words.

2. True or False: If you want to know if a source is credible, check whether their publisher has a reputation for being trustworthy.

3. True or False: We don't always have to cite a source when we use someone else's ideas, just when we use the biggest ones.

4. True or false: You can't draw evidence to support an argument from a literary source because they're not true.

5. True or false: If you've got a credible source, you only need one.

6. True or false: You can only draw evidence from printed sources, not the Internet or television.

7. Is this a good research question? Why or why not? What time do the stars usually appear in the sky over Denver in mid-July?

8. You are working on a paper about the images taken by the Hubble Telescope this year. List three possible sources.

9. You are working on a research paper on how Emily Dickinson writes about rain in her poetry. Would a news article about a Dickinson family reunion written by a distant relative be a good source for the paper? Why or why not?

10. Choose a current event in the news and research the accounts of two people who were actually there and saw it happen. Then write a brief paragraph comparing and contrasting their accounts.

ANSWERS

CHECK YOUR ANSWERS

1. False

2. True

3. False

4. False

5. False

6. False

7. No. It is so narrow in focus that it does not allow room for discussion and analysis.

8. Recent published articles about the Hubble Telescope, public images from the Hubble Telescope, and the official Hubble Telescope website

9. Probably not, unless those memories relate directly to rain

10. Both Mike Chang and Tabitha Jones attended the recent speech of a visiting politician. Both of them mention how passionate the politician became when discussing education, and they both state that he said he used to stay up all night to finish his favorite books. However, Mike's description focuses on the audience, because he was surprised to see so many young people in the crowd. Tabitha spent more time talking about the politician's arguments. She agreed with him that more resources should go to schools, but she wished he had spent more time talking about the importance of the arts in schools, too.

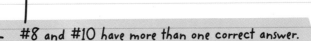

#8 and #10 have more than one correct answer.

Chapter 29

WRITING PRACTICES

Development

You want to write something, but where do you start? You start with **DEVELOPMENT**. There are two stages of development:

1. Planning: laying the initial plans

2. Revising your plan: going over the initial plans and making any necessary changes

> **DEVELOPMENT**
> the planning that goes into a writing project before you begin writing

There are three questions to think about to develop an idea:

1. TASK: What do you want to write? (Or what have you been assigned to write?)

EXAMPLE: writing a business plan for your soccer team fund-raiser

---

2. PURPOSE: Why do you want to write it?

EXAMPLE: to get enough money from your friends, family, and community to rent a van to travel to a state competition

---

3. AUDIENCE: Who are you writing to?

EXAMPLE: your friends, family, community, and local business owners

> Just think of these three question words when you are in development to focus your task, purpose, and audience:
> **WHAT?**
> **WHY?**
> **WHO?**

You may even want to jot down the answers to these questions before starting to write. You can keep the answers in front of you as a reminder of what you must write.

Audience

Your audience is the people you are writing to who will (hopefully) read what you've written. If you're a journalist at a local

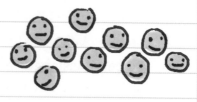

newspaper, you may write for your community. If you're a mystery writer, you may write for all people who love mysteries.

Once you know your audience, ask these questions:

* Does the audience know everything you know? Your audience may not be familiar with all the people, places, things, or ideas that you know. If they aren't, you need to introduce and explain these new things. But if your audience is familiar or the information is common knowledge, you don't need to spend time on the concepts.

* Does the audience feel the same way you do? If the audience doesn't agree with you, you may need to spend some time making your argument.

* Does the audience expect something specific from you? If you're writing for a very specific task, purpose, or audience, then it doesn't make sense to write something that doesn't fit readers' expectations.

If you're at a poetry reading, the audience will be very confused if you start reading a political speech. Or vice versa—if you start reading poetry at a political rally, the audience will be confused, because what you're saying doesn't meet their expectations. Instead of focusing on your message, the audience would focus on how the poem is out of place.

PLANNING
Brainstorming

As you start to answer all these questions, you're planning— all the thinking you do before you actually start putting anything on paper or on the screen. But just because you're not creating finished sentences doesn't mean you're not writing. Planning is a crucial part of the writing process.

One tool you can use in the planning stage is **BRAINSTORMING**. Once you come up with a topic, you'll start to get ideas and questions. Some of them will be good, and some of them won't be so good. Some of them will be on topic, and some of them might not connect as well. But in brainstorming, you don't try to figure that all out, you just try to get it all down. Take some time when you're in the planning stages just to write

> **BRAINSTORM**
> produce ideas

down whatever comes into your head. That's brainstorming. Once you've got it all down, you can start to think about what you want to focus on, what you want to eliminate, or what other ideas you come up with!

Organization

Once you develop your ideas, you need to organize them in order to plan what to write. To do that, look back at your answers to the task, purpose, and audience questions:

Task: <u>What</u> do you want to do? Organize your piece to best suit your task.

> **EXAMPLE:** A fictional short story and a newspaper article don't start out the same way. They're organized differently. A news article puts the most important things at the beginning. A fictional short story can have a lot of different structures, but often it has the most important action toward the end. Align your organizational structure to your task.

Purpose: Why do you want to do it? Organize your information to best suit your purpose.

EXAMPLE: In a news article, you want to get the news to everybody as quickly as possible. That's why it's organized with the most important information at the beginning. In a fictional short story, an author can have a lot of different purposes—if he or she wants to express an idea, the author may weave the idea throughout the story. If the author wants to write a mystery, he or she probably won't reveal the most important information until the very end, so there is suspense throughout.

Audience: Who are you writing to? Organize your information to best suit your audience.

EXAMPLE: Different audiences prefer different organization. If you want to explain a scientific concept to a group of scientists, you might organize your thoughts in the format that they are familiar with—perhaps like a standard scientific paper, with an introduction, argument, and conclusions. But if you want to explain that same idea to a group of first graders, you might organize it as a story, with a beginning, middle, and end, so you can keep their attention.

Outlining

An outline is like the road map to your piece. In it, you capture:

All the things you want to say

The order in which you want to say them

Brainstorming gets all your ideas down on paper.

Organizing helps you think about the best way to get your ideas across: where to start, how to get your points across, and where you want to wind up.

Outlining gives you a place to note all those thoughts down, using main headings for the big ideas and subheadings for your supporting details.

TITLE: Why Public Gardens Are Important

INTRODUCTION: Claim and brief history of public
   gardens
   - Claim: Public gardens are important parts
     of our society.
   - The first public gardens
   - How the craze grew
   - Public gardens in the present

Reason Why Public Gardens Are Important: Health
   - Physical health benefits of public gardens
   - Mental health benefits of public gardens

Reason Why Public Gardens Are Important: Community
   - Community is built by working in gardens.
   - Community is built by visiting gardens.

CONCLUSION: Public gardens should be supported
   in the future.
   - Recap of importance
   - Plans for the future

Revising Your Outline

Once you have written your outline, review everything. Ask yourself the same questions you started out with, then ask yourself if you've accomplished what you set out to.

Task: What did I want to say? Have I said it?

Purpose: Why did I want to write about this? Have I accomplished what I meant to?

Audience: Who is my audience? Have I planned points that will connect with them?

Organization: How is this organized? Is this the best way to present my ideas?

Completion: Are these thoughts complete? Is anything missing?

Now, you're ready to write a **DRAFT**!

> **DRAFT**
> a preliminary version of a piece of writing

REVISING the FIRST DRAFT

Once your first draft is finished, there's still a little more work to do—first you have to **EDIT** and revise it so it's better.

> **EDIT**
> to correct, condense, or make changes to a text

To edit and revise, we use the same three questions we started with, on task, purpose, and audience.

> No two people revise the same way, so ask your teacher how he or she revises—you may find a new method that works better for you!

First, reread your piece and revise only for task, purpose, and audience:

TASK: Did I do what I was supposed to do here?

PURPOSE: Did I do it for the reasons I was supposed to?

AUDIENCE: Did I write it in a way that my audience will understand and respond to?

Second, reread your piece and revise only for CLARITY and STRENGTH. Does it make sense? Will the reader understand your writing? Does it have the best ideas and strongest evidence?

Last, reread your piece and revise only for GRAMMAR and PUNCTUATION. Using correct grammar and punctuation is an important part of writing and revising. Grammar and punctuation are like signs that tell the reader how to read. For example, a period is like a big stop sign. Without the right grammar and punctuation, the reader can easily get lost.

EXAMPLE:
TASK, PURPOSE, AND AUDIENCE:

Also reread your writing aloud (to yourself or to someone else). Hearing the words spoken aloud can help to highlight what needs to be edited!

If you are writing a business plan for your soccer team fund-raiser, maybe at first you thought you wouldn't bother to include information about competing soccer teams. But then you realize that your audience—

your friends, family, and community—don't know that you're neck and neck with another team and are very close to becoming champions of the state, which is why it's really important you get to the competition. That means you probably need to add a section about the competing soccer teams and your own team's rank.

CLARITY AND STRENGTH: Once you add that section, read the whole thing over again, making sure that your sentences are clear and that you've used all your best ideas and all the strongest evidence you can find. Wait! You realize that you didn't offer any evidence to prove how much you believe you can raise this year, so you dig up the amount raised last year to prove that this year's goal is possible.

GRAMMAR AND PUNCTUATION: Finally, you go over the nitty-gritty details. You turn a run-on sentence into two proper sentences. You capitalize your coach's name, which had somehow slipped through the cracks. You make sure that the rest of the grammar and punctuation is perfect. Finally, you've got a finished draft!

STYLE

STYLE is simply the way in which something is written—it is not the idea or thing being expressed. You can express the same idea in completely different styles.

EXAMPLE:

> Many people who grew up in the Blue Ridge Mountains believe, secretly or not so secretly, that they may be the most beautiful mountains in the world.

 The style of this writing is SLIGHTLY FORMAL and conveys respect for the people of the Blue Ridge Mountains and their opinions.

EXAMPLE:

> Those people from the Blue Ridge Mountains all seem to think they've got the most beautiful mountain range in the world.

 The style of this writing is more INFORMAL, almost sarcastic, and conveys a bit of disrespect for the people of the Blue Ridge Mountains and their opinions.

The information in the sentence stays pretty much the same, but the styles of the sentences are completely different. Style can influence the audience's impression of what is being expressed. When you write or revise your writing, you want to choose a style that's appropriate for your . . .

Task!

Purpose!

Audience!

↑
YOU GUESSED IT!

Task:

Does the style help you do what you're supposed to do? If you're writing a news article, does it fit the style of a news article? If you're writing a scientific paper, does it fit the style of a scientific paper?

EXAMPLE:

A well-written speech that is appropriately formal:

> "Ladies and gentlemen, I am delighted to take the podium and deliver my new paper on the behavior patterns of the Bermuda glowfish to this distinguished audience."

A badly written speech that is inappropriately informal:

> "Hey! It's so cool so many of you are out here today! Thanks a lot for coming. I've just got this paper here I was going to read to you. It's about some stuff I found out while I was doing research on the Bermuda glowfish. . . ."

Purpose:

Does the style help accomplish the purpose of the task?

Does the style help get the argument across?

Does it help tell the story better?

EXAMPLE:

A well-written recipe that makes each step clear:

Mix together the wet ingredients: eggs, butter, oil, and vanilla. Then sift together the dry ingredients: flour, baking soda, sugar, and cocoa powder. Pour the dry ingredients slowly into the mixture of wet ingredients, mixing thoroughly, until a batter forms.

A badly written recipe that is too wordy and confusing:

With an artisan's careful touch, mix the cracked eggs, the luscious butter, the translucent oil, and the delicious vanilla together. The dry ingredients will then get equal treatment, being sifted together in a fine dust of flour cracked from golden wheat, baking soda to lend punch, the sweetness of sugar, and the mysterious bitterness of cocoa powder. . . .

Audience:

Does the style help you connect with the audience? Is it the style they expect to hear? Is it the style they're most likely to listen to?

EXAMPLE:

A well-written story that is entertaining and lively:

> When Jonathan Gulliver woke up, he was afraid that it was going to be another boring day. But when he got up and opened his closet door, he got the surprise of his life.

A badly written story that is <u>dry and hard to follow</u>:

> Jonathan Gulliver was bored. The day before had been boring, and the day before that had been boring. There was no reason, his groggy mind thought, as he painfully woke from a very, very, very deep slumber, that today should be any different than the day before and the day before that. He opened his chest door and something surprised him.

Grammar and Punctuation for Style

These are a few tools that can add to the style of your piece:

PARENTHETICAL ELEMENTS

PARENTHETICAL ELEMENTS are things that aren't essential to a sentence but that you want to mention along the way. There are three main ways to punctuate them:

〉 Commas can be used where you want to introduce a slight interruption.

COMMA EXAMPLE:

The whole gymnasium, which was the size of two basketball courts, was filled with soap bubbles.

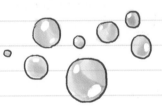

( ) Parentheses are like commas, but they put a bit more emphasis on what's inside them.

PARENTHESES EXAMPLE:

The whole gymnasium (which had been filled with soap bubbles) was impossible to use.

▭ Dashes give even more emphasis to what's between them than commas or parentheses. Use them when you really want someone to pay attention.

DASHES EXAMPLE:

The whole gymnasium—which had been a gift to the school only the year before—was filled with soap bubbles as a senior prank.

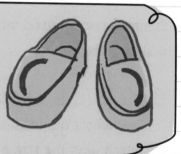

Sometimes you can use just one comma or just one dash— but you can never use just one parenthesis. They ALWAYS come in pairs.

PUNCTUATION, PAUSES, AND BREAKS

Commas and dashes aren't just good for adding a little extra information to a sentence. Sometimes we can use them when we want to take a little break in the action.

COMMA EXAMPLE:

The game was long, but exciting.

DASH EXAMPLE:

Jessica thought the game was over—until the score was tied at the last minute.

There's another way to take a break in a sentence as well . . . the **ELLIPSIS**.

> **ELLIPSIS**
> three evenly spaced dots that indicate a pause or an omission

The ellipsis isn't just for pauses. It can also be used to indicate that something is (MISSING) from a sentence. For example, if someone starts to say something but doesn't finish.

ELLIPSIS EXAMPLE:

I wish . . . but that doesn't matter now.

Or if we are quoting something that someone else wrote, but we don't want to quote the whole thing.

ELLIPSIS EXAMPLE:

Original quotation: "The whole team, who had been through all 50 states and managed to track down a pepperoni pizza in every one they visited, was glad to be home."

Quotation with ellipsis: "The whole team . . . was glad to be home."

The ellipsis makes the quote simpler and gets the main point across more quickly.

Style Tips

KEEP IT CONSISTENT

Good style is consistent. That means it doesn't change in tone from sentence to sentence or from beginning to end.

CONSISTENT TONE EXAMPLE:

> I believe it is time for all good people to come to the aid of the parade float committee. Now is the time for us to accomplish this considerable and worthy task.

If you start out in a formal style, stay formal. (Or if you start out in an informal style, stay informal.) <u>Switching from style to style can be pretty jarring for your audience.</u>

INCONSISTENT TONE EXAMPLE:

> Hey, y'all! Now is the time for us to accomplish this considerable and worthy task—making some awesome floats!

DON'T BORE YOUR READER

Style should be consistent, but you don't want to write the same type of sentence over and over.

REPETITIVE SENTENCE STRUCTURE EXAMPLE:

> I went to the store. I got a carton of milk. I got a loaf of bread. I walked home.

That's pretty boring. Instead, use VARIED SENTENCE PATTERNS by changing the styles in your sentences.

VARIED SENTENCE STRUCTURE EXAMPLE:

I went to the store, where I got a carton of milk. Then I got a loaf of bread. Finally, I went home.

That's a lot more interesting to read than the previous example. You can also vary sentences to emphasize your meaning, like this:

EXAMPLE:

I went to the store, because I was quite hungry. I picked out a loaf of bread, and then realized that I was also thirsty. So I also snapped up a carton of milk before I went home.

The original version doesn't explain WHY the author did anything, but this version adds quite a bit of meaning to explain why the author bought the things he or she did. The original version also makes everything seem equally important, because all the sentences are the same. But this sentence structure shows that being hungry and thirsty, and buying food and drink, are the most important parts of the story.

AVOID WORDINESS AND REDUNDANCY

WORDINESS is using an excessive number of words. It's best to keep things short, so each word has a big impact.

WORDY EXAMPLE:

"He's an extraordinary contortionist and the best at his craft. There's no contortionist as remarkable in history."

When we use unnecessary words, the sentence loses its impact and your reader can get lost or bored. Solution: Make sure you don't use unnecessary words.

CONCISE EXAMPLE:

"He was the most extraordinary contortionist who ever lived."

Your audience isn't likely to forget that any time soon!

REDUNDANCY is including words that could be omitted without losing the meaning of the passage.

REDUNDANT EXAMPLE:

"She's the most wonderful, amazing, perfect, fantastic, unbelievable, extraordinary, marvelous runner I've ever seen."

When we pile words up on each other—especially when they mean similar things—they tend to lose their impact and meaning. Solution: Pick just a few precise words.

PRECISE EXAMPLE:

"She's the most extraordinary runner I've ever seen."

That's a statement your audience will remember!

extraordinary!

COLLABORATION
people working together

You don't have to do all your writing and thinking alone. **COLLABORATION** takes advantage of the fact that two heads are better than one. Working with others can help at every stage of the game. Another writer can help you with everything from coming up with ideas at the beginning to editing at the end. It works both ways— you can also help them!

Publishing

Once you write something, you want to share it with the
world. How do you do that? By publishing it! There are many
ways to publish your writing for different audiences:

School publications share your work
with classmates and teachers.

Local publications share your work
with your local community.

Commercial publishers share your work
around the world.

Self-publishing allows you to publish your work
yourself and share with whomever you like.

In each of these categories, you can publish your writing in many different mediums:

* News outlets

* Magazines

* Books

* Internet publications

* Blogs

CHECK YOUR KNOWLEDGE

1. True or false: An ellipsis can indicate a pause or an omission in a sentence.

2. When you work with another writer, what is it called?

3. Define "style."

4. What three things do we need to keep in mind at every stage of writing?

5. List some ways to add style to your writing with punctuation.

6. What do we call making changes to existing text?

7. Should you develop your ideas first or organize your ideas first?

8. True or false: The style of all your sentences should be the same.

9. Develop an idea for a short essay based on this prompt: Can computer games be used effectively as an educational tool in the classroom?

10. Write an outline based on your ideas for the previous prompt.

ANSWERS

1. True

2. Collaboration

3. Style is the way something is written.

4. Task, purpose, audience

5. By using parenthetical elements with commas, parentheses, or dashes. Also, by breaking up sentences with ellipsis.

6. Editing

7. Develop

8. False

9. A computer game that allows kids to fly planes across international boundaries, land, and explore those countries virtually could be used as an educational tool in classes on culture and geography.

10. Introduction

Pose question: Can computer games educate?
Answer: Yes

Benefits of the International Geography and
Culture Game:

Gets and keeps kids' Attention

Teaches Culture

Teaches Geography

Conclusion:
Restate question: Can computer games educate?
Restate benefits

#5, #9, and #10 have more than one correct answer.

Chapter 30

WRITING ARGUMENTS

ARGUMENTATIVE WRITING takes a position and supports it with reason and evidence. An argument consists of:

CLAIM:
the point you want to prove

EVIDENCE:
facts that support your argument

REASON:
logic that connects the evidence to your argument

COUNTERCLAIMS:
claims that contradict your claim

CONCLUSION:
the summary of your argument or the final judgment you've reached through your argument

ORGANIZATION

Organization helps you structure your writing so it's as persuasive as possible. In an argument, the order matters a lot. If you start giving evidence before you state your claim, people may not know what you're trying to prove. If you state your reasons before you give your evidence, people may think that you're just making up claims, without any facts to support them. To make an effective argument, everything needs to be in the right order, with your claims supported by evidence and reasons, and all of it leading up to your logical conclusion.

ORGANIZED EXAMPLE: INTRODUCTION

Everyone knows that studying helps you learn.
But exercising your body is as important as ← CLAIM
exercising your mind. In fact, kids who exercise
more do better on tests—even when they don't
study any more than other kids. People who do ⟩ EVIDENCE
some gentle exercise as they're listening to new
information tend to remember it better.
So if you want to learn more, and learn ← CONCLUSION
better, don't just hit the books—get moving!

But when we scramble the sentences, it makes much less sense!

VS.

UNORGANIZED EXAMPLE:

People who do some gentle exercise as they're listening to new information tend to remember it better. But exercising your body is as important as exercising your mind. Everyone knows that studying helps you learn. So if you want to learn more, and learn better, don't just hit the books—get moving! In fact, kids who exercise more do better on tests—even when they don't study any more than other kids.

Without the introduction, we don't understand how this fact connects to anything.

Without the introduction, we don't understand what this claim relates to.

This conclusion hasn't been proven yet because the earlier sentences are confusing and out of order . . . and there's another sentence after it.

This isn't a conclusion, it's a piece of evidence. It doesn't make sense to leave it here, after the argument has already been made.

The sentences are in random order, so you can barely tell what the author is saying! Even when all the right pieces are there, they won't get your point across unless they're in the right order.

435

Transitions

When writing an argument, certain words can signal the relationship between your claims, reasons, evidence, counterclaims, and conclusion—they are called TRANSITION WORDS or PHRASES. These are some common ones:

Evidence: These words signal that the author is connecting a piece of evidence to a piece of reasoning or a claim:

Due to	Specifically
For example	After all
For instance	To illustrate

Reasons: These words signal that the author is connecting a previously mentioned piece of evidence to a claim or conclusion:

Therefore

So

Because

For

Thus

In other words

Counterclaims: These words signal that the author is connecting a counterclaim to a previously explained concept, why he or she disagrees with a counterclaim, or how a counterclaim is connected to his or her own argument:

One might argue

Nevertheless

But

Otherwise

However

Though

Rather

Yet

In contrast

On the other hand

Conclusion: These words signal that the author is connecting all of the previous information to a final conclusion:

As a result

Hence

Finally

In conclusion

Last

Transitional phrases are like road maps through an argument. They can also help us within each section of an argument to communicate things like:

More to come:

Next

Besides

Furthermore

Finally

In addition

Still

Moreover

Likewise

And

Similarly

Also

Change ahead:

Although

Nevertheless

However

Otherwise

Yet

Instead

Important ideas:

Above all

Most important

The main concern

Order or sequence:

First

Eventually

Second

Since

Third

Earlier

Next

Before

In addition

Now

Afterward

Meanwhile

STEPS to BUILDING an ARGUMENT
Introduce Your Claims

The most important thing in an argument is to make sure everyone knows what your main point is. Clearly state your claim—nobody can agree with you if they don't know what you're saying.

UNCLEAR EXAMPLE:

We still need regular books, even with computers.

This claim isn't focused enough to be clear. The author hasn't explained what "regular" means. The category of "computers" is too broad to be meaningful.

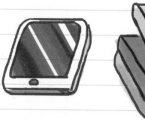

CLEAR EXAMPLE:

Digital books may be catching on, but readers still want printed books.

This claim is clear and focused. It draws a clear distinction between digital books and printed books, and also explains what the author believes about both.

Support Your Claims

You don't have a strong argument if you don't support your claims. To do so, you need to write clear reasons and support them with relevant evidence. <u>Include facts</u> that support your claim, and don't include information that isn't connected to your argument. Also, always cite your sources!

EXAMPLE:

Readers still desire printed books.

RELEVANT EVIDENCE:

Printed book sales dropped when digital readers were introduced, but now sales of traditional books are rising again (Gibson, "E-books Go Out of Fashion as Book Sales Revive." TIME. 2015).

IRRELEVANT EVIDENCE:

Printed books can be used as doorstops.

Doesn't connect with the "readers" part of the argument because a book used as a doorstop is not being read.

Evidence and reason are closely related, but they're not the same. Evidence answers the question "What makes you think that?" Reason answers the question "Why is that important?"

EXAMPLE:

Claim:

My team will win the state championship this year.

Evidence/What makes you think that?

We have a great running game, a fabulous defense, and strong players.

Reasons/Why is that important?

The last team to win the state championship had the exact same characteristics.

You must always connect your evidence to reasoning for a strong explanation. Otherwise, your evidence won't support your argument well.

EXAMPLE:

CLAIM

I don't think it's a good idea to picnic today. It's raining.

EVIDENCE

The rain is a fact about the world, but by itself, it's not a reason for something. A reason connects your evidence to your argument.

EXAMPLE:

CLAIM

I don't think it's a good idea to picnic today.

It's raining, so we will get wet if we are outside.

EVIDENCE   REASON

ACKNOWLEDGE ALTERNATE AND OPPOSING CLAIMS

You can't win an argument by pretending no one disagrees with you—then you leave your argument open to readers pointing out obvious counterclaims. You've got to acknowledge those disagreements and REFUTE them, or prove them wrong.
Simply include the opposing claim and write a **REBUTTAL**, or reason why the claim isn't valid.

> **REBUTTAL**
> contradiction

EXAMPLE:

COUNTERCLAIM

Some people say that as the world becomes increasingly dependent on digital devices, the printed book will eventually become a thing of the past. But digital technology is still new, while the technology of the printed book has persisted for thousands of years. As the world becomes increasingly digital, people have also begun to long for things that they can see, touch, and enjoy in the real world—like printed books.

REBUTTAL

COME TO A CONCLUSION

When you get to the end, it's time to wrap it all up with CONCLUDING STATEMENTS. A concluding statement should restate your argument or claim and summarize the most important points covered in the passage.

EXAMPLE:

Given the fact that the printed book has survived enormous cultural changes over thousands of years and the fact that readers today are buying more of them than before, it's clear that the printed book is here to stay.

1. What are the five parts of an argument?

2. True or false: It doesn't really matter what order you put your claims, reasons, and evidence in.

3. True or false: A counterclaim supports the original claim.

4. True or false: It's fine to introduce evidence without offering reasons why it connects to the original claim.

5. List three words that can signal a conclusion.

6. True or false: It's not important to clearly introduce your claims, because people will start to understand them over the course of your argument.

7. Think of an argument you want to make to your neighbors and write a clear claim for it.

8. Outline your argument, making sure you include all five necessary elements.

9. Write your argument as a short paragraph to be given as a speech to other students.

10. Write your argument as several paragraphs to be published as an opinion article.

CHECK YOUR ANSWERS

1. A claim, evidence, reason, counterclaims, and a conclusion

2. False

3. False

4. False

5. As a result, Hence, Finally

6. False

> #7 through #10 have more than one correct answer.

7. It's important to shop at locally owned businesses.

8. Introduction: Big chains now cover the United States.

   Claim: But it's important to shop at locally owned businesses.

   Reason/Evidence: It builds connections between people in a community. Studies show people feel more connected with each other when they shop locally.

Reason/Evidence: It strengthens the economy of our community. Economic indicators show that the community's financial strength grows when people shop locally.

Counterclaim: Chain stores can create jobs and the ability to buy new products.

Rebuttal: Most people in the community will only spend their money in the new store—not get jobs—so more money will go to a distant corporation than come into the community. Also, products from chain stores are generic—they aren't as unique as locally made crafts and products.

Reason/Evidence: It gives us a richer culture everywhere. More local businesses mean more interesting options for everyone.

Conclusion: We should shop at locally owned businesses.

9. Big chain stores now cover the United States. But that just means it's more important than ever to shop locally. When we shop locally, we build our community. Studies show that people feel more connected with one another when they shop locally. We also strengthen our community's economic base, as revealed by economic indicators that show a community's financial position improves when its members

shop locally. Some say chain stores can bring jobs to a town, but the majority of people in the community will only shop in these stores, and that means more money will go to a distant corporation than come into the community. Finally, we make the whole world a more interesting place. The culture of the entire country is enriched when different local communities support their own special trades, crafts, and products. So let's all shop locally!

10. Big chain stores now cover the country, offering many of the same products in every state. But that just means it's more important than ever to shop locally to strengthen our community.

When we shop locally, we build connections between people in our community. We get to know the store owners and their stories, and they get to know ours. We run into friends and neighbors who are also shopping at local stores. Studies show that people feel more connected with each other when they shop locally.

We also strengthen our community's economic base by supporting local businesses. Some argue that if chain stores are blocked from entering a community, the community won't get those jobs. Although a chain can employ some people, the majority of people in the community will only shop at the chain. Therefore, more money will go to a distant corporation than come into the community. When we shop locally, the money we spend stays in the community, in the hands of our friends and neighbors, who often put it right back into our own community. So it's no wonder that economic indicators show that a community's financial position improves when its members shop locally.

Finally, we make the whole world a more interesting place when we shop at local businesses. It's a lot more interesting to stop to get peach cider in South Carolina and local chili in Cincinnati than it is to eat at the same fast-food place everywhere we go. Who wants generic products from chain stores when there are unique locally made crafts and products? The culture of the entire country is enriched when different local communities support their own special trades, crafts, and products.

Shopping locally: It strengthens our economy, our bonds with one another, and the culture of the whole country. That just makes sense.

Chapter 31

EXPOSITORY WRITING: INFORMATIVE AND EXPLANATORY TEXTS

EXPOSITORY WRITING is writing text that informs, describes, and explains. There are two main types:

1. INFORMATIVE WRITING

conveys information. It's writing that tells you about something. If you know a lot about birds, stars, baseball . . . or anything else, and you'd like to share that knowledge with others, you want to do some informative writing.

2. EXPLANATORY WRITING

offers explanations. It's writing that answers a question like, "How does this thing work?" Or "Why is that thing like that?" If you want to explain why the sky is blue, or how to fix a bike, or why Friday is called Friday, you'll do some explanatory writing.

ORGANIZATION

There are many ways to organize informative or explanatory writing. Some common strategies include:

DEFINITION:

Define and thoroughly describe your subject, giving details that help the reader understand what it is.

EXAMPLE:

an essay defining the life cycle

CLASSIFICATION:

Explain how your subject relates to other subjects, helping the reader understand where it fits into the broader scheme of things.

EXAMPLE:

an encyclopedia entry explaining how one species of seagull relates to all other species of seagulls around the world

COMPARISON/CONTRAST:

Describe the similarities and the differences between two subjects.

EXAMPLE:

a history book that compares the way two different presidents led the country during a time of economic pressure, describing how they faced similar circumstances but responded to them differently

CAUSE/EFFECT:

Focus on the causes behind events and their consequences.

EXAMPLE:

a speech that lets kids know that if they begin to save small sums of money now, the interest on their savings will grow over time and provide them with more freedom when they get older

Once you have your overall structure, you can help get your point across by using other elements of organization, such as:

FORMATTING:

Headers, or section titles, that let people know where they are and what's coming next

THIS IS A HEADER!!

457

GRAPHICS:

Charts and tables that show information visually or can display information that supports the text

EXAMPLE:

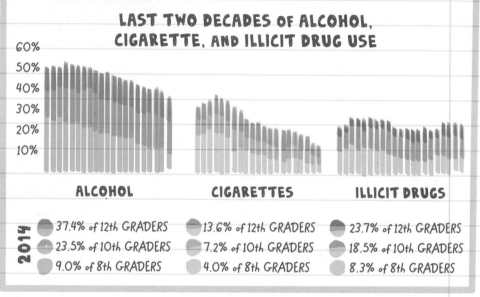

LAST TWO DECADES OF ALCOHOL, CIGARETTE, AND ILLICIT DRUG USE

ALCOHOL
- 37.4% of 12th GRADERS
- 23.5% of 10th GRADERS
- 9.0% of 8th GRADERS

CIGARETTES
- 13.6% of 12th GRADERS
- 7.2% of 10th GRADERS
- 4.0% of 8th GRADERS

ILLICIT DRUGS
- 23.7% of 12th GRADERS
- 18.5% of 10th GRADERS
- 8.3% of 8th GRADERS

2014

MULTIMEDIA:

Depending on what you are writing, you may be able to include audio or video to help illustrate a point.

EXAMPLE:

If you are writing a blog post on the medicinal plants found in the Amazon, you may want to link to a video of a shaman discussing the power of a plant from the rain forest.

Introducing the Topic

In informative writing, an introduction is like a preview of what you will explain or describe. It gives the reader a glimpse of what's going to come next.

EXAMPLE:

People have been staring up at the moon, making guesses about what it must be like up there, for centuries. But it's only in the past few decades that astronomers and astronauts have begun to find solid scientific answers to that question.

Developing the Topic

After the introduction, the topic is developed with relevant facts and pieces of information that directly relate to the topic.

EXAMPLE:

Relevant: Astronauts were surprised to find out that because of the lack of atmosphere, shadows on the moon are much darker than they are on Earth.

Not Relevant: Everyone from poets to pop stars has written about what it might be like to spend time on the moon.

The most common way of developing an informative or explanatory text is to include:

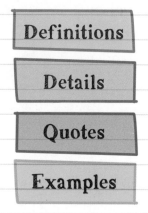

Definitions

Details

Quotes

Examples

When you include definitions, details, or examples it also helps to precisely describe the nature of the subjects discussed.

IMPRECISE EXAMPLE:

A moonquake is a shaking fit experienced by the moon.

Adding details can offer additional relevant information, break down tricky concepts into more manageable chunks, or expand the reader's understanding of a point.

PRECISE EXAMPLE:

There are four kinds of moonquakes: those caused by meteor impacts, those caused by the heat of the sun, and those caused by internal geological shifts—some shallow, and some deep.

Quotes, which report direct speech or language written by other writers, can add a first-hand account, build on information given, and offer a second verification of facts.

EXAMPLE:

Shallow moonquakes can cause a lot of motion on the surface of the moon and a lot of noise. According to Professor Clive Neal, who studies the data from the original Apollo moon landings, during some moonquakes, "The moon was ringing like a bell."

Examples can offer an illustration of the topic under discussion.

EXAMPLE:

Lunar dust, which is very fine and very rough, is a big threat to astronauts on the moon. For instance, it can scratch visors so badly that astronauts can barely see through them. Lunar dust has been known to almost completely disintegrate moon boots.

Making a Conclusion

In informative or explanatory writing, concluding statements summarize the information that was presented. However, you should not simply repeat exactly what you wrote previously—you should find a new way to restate the information that brings it all together and highlights the most important points.

EXAMPLE:

Poets and pop stars might have thought there would be no need to dream about the moon after astronauts brought back reports from the surface. But with super-dark shadows, moonquakes, and strange lunar dust, there's even more to dream about than ever before.

Conclusions can also invite the reader to get involved in the topic—like at the end of a persuasive piece or argument. They can suggest further steps to learn more, too, such as in informative texts.

USE JUST the RIGHT WORDS
Transitional Phrases and Signal Words

You can use all the transitional phrases and signal words you use in writing arguments to write informative and explanatory texts, too. But instead of their job being to transition between claims, reasons, and evidence, they will show the relationship between ideas and information.

Domain-Specific Vocabulary

DOMAIN-SPECIFIC VOCABULARY are words that are used for a particular topic. Certain professions and groups use special vocabularies, which are called **JARGON**. Doctors use medical jargon. Lawyers use legal jargon. Engineers and computer programmers use technical jargon. If you write about a world that uses jargon, you can use their domain-specific vocabulary.

However, be careful with jargon! Your audience may not know domain-specific words. If the vocabulary is not common knowledge, explain the word or phrase's meaning.

EXAMPLE:

The carnival workers would sometimes enjoy an "aba-daba"— carnival lingo for dessert cooked up in the carnival cookhouse—before going to bed.

EXAMPLE:

When a lawyer says she's going to "execute" a document, it doesn't mean that anyone needs to fear for his or her life. In legal jargon, to "execute" something means to sign something, complete a task, or carry out an agreement.

CHECK YOUR KNOWLEDGE

1. What illustrates an idea or concept?

2. True or false: Because informative writing is about sharing information, it's good to include as many facts as possible, even if they're not relevant.

3. What do you call an organizational style that explains where a subject fits in among other subjects?

4. True or false: Charts can't be used to help your readers comprehend your point.

5. True or false: In informative writing, the introduction serves as a preview of what's to come.

6. True or false: If you use jargon, don't waste time explaining it to your audience.

7. Choose a topic you'd like to know more about. Do some research, and write three facts about it that you didn't know before.

8. Use your research to write a brief informative piece, with an introductory sentence, facts, explanations, and a conclusion.

9. Think of a dish that you don't know how to cook. Do some research, then write notes on how to create it.

10. Based on the dish you researched, write a brief explanatory piece, with an introductory sentence and a conclusion, that shares that explanation.

CHECK YOUR ANSWERS

1. An example

2. False

3. Classification

4. False

5. True

6. False

#7 through #10 have more than one correct answer.

7. What is the world's tallest dog? The Great Dane. The current record is held by a dog named Zeus, who stands 44 inches tall. Great Danes were bred by Germans to hunt boar. They are obedient and love to do things with their owners.

8. There are a lot of dog breeds that grow quite tall, but the tallest dog in the world is a Great Dane named Zeus, who stands 44 inches tall. Great Danes were bred by Germans to hunt boar, so they needed to be big.

But, they're very obedient and love to do things with their owners. They also make good pets—even if some of them might be taller than their owners!

9. How to make mozzarella cheese:

1) Add citric acid and water to cold milk.

2) Heat up the milk, then take it off the heat.

3) Add rennet (curdled milk) and wait for curds to form, then cut the curds.

4) Heat the curds back up, then take them off the burner and separate the curds and whey (a watery liquid).

5) Knead the curds until they become like dough.

6) Stretch the curds, then form the cheese back into a ball.

10. Mozzarella cheese is delicious and easy to make at home with just a few simple ingredients. The process starts with a gallon of cold milk. Citric acid and water are added to the milk, which is then heated. When the mixture is hot, rennet (curdled milk) is added to form curds. Once curds ➡

form, they're cut and heated again. Then the white curds, which will become cheese, are separated from the whey, a watery liquid. The curds are kneaded together until they become like dough, then are stretched to give the mozzarella its texture. Finally, the cheese is shaped back into a smooth sphere that is ready to eat—and delicious.

Chapter 32

WRITING NARRATIVES

A **NARRATIVE** is a description of events that are connected to each other—also known as a story. Fiction writers use narrative to describe imaginary events, but interesting stories happen in real life, too. Nonfiction writers use narrative to describe real events. Just like any good story, a good narrative has a beginning, middle, and end. Narratives also contain these elements:

Context and/or setting

A point of view

Characters or actors

Plot

Conclusion

Put these together, and you've got all the elements of a story—whether it's fictional or true.

CONTEXT and/or SETTING

Readers often need both **CONTEXT** and **SETTING** to orient them in a story and understand it. The context of a narrative is:

> What else is happening at the same time as the story

> What happened before the story begins that is important for the reader to know so he understands the story

The setting of a narrative is:

> When a story happens

> Where a story happens

EXAMPLE:

CONTEXT

Winter was always tough in the tiny village of Della Gloria, because every year the mountain snow cuts it off from the big town in the valley below.

But the winter after the war
ended was especially bad.

SETTING

How to Create a Setting

Answer these questions to begin creating a vivid time
and place:

What does the setting look like?

What does the setting sound like?

What does it feel like to be there?

**What is the historical time and place
of the setting?**

What is going on in the world at that time?

NARRATION

In a fictional story, the story is told from the point of view of the narrator. Authors often choose from the three most common types of narrators in fiction:

First-person narrator: a narrator who is also a character in the story. Authors might use first-person narration if the character of the narrator is important to the story or if the story is best told from a single point of view.

Second-person narrator: tells the story as if it is happening to "you." Authors use second-person narration if they want readers to strongly relate and react to the story.

Third-person narrator: a narrator who is not a character in the story. Authors use third-person narration if they want to explore the points of view of many characters or tell a story that doesn't focus on a narrator's character.

A few more things to consider when thinking about narration style:

A subjective narrative style concentrates on the feelings and opinions of the narrator.

EXAMPLE:

It was the most beautiful thing in the world when the surf filled with incredible tiny glowing fish on the first night in August.

An objective narrative style conveys the facts with no opinions or slant.

EXAMPLE:

On the first night in August, the surf filled with tiny glowing fish.

A TRUSTWORTHY NARRATOR conveys facts and opinions that turn out to be true over the course of the story.

EXAMPLE:

A narrator tells you at the beginning of the story that he is a doctor, and all of the events of the story confirm that he is.

An UNTRUSTWORTHY NARRATOR conveys facts and opinions that turn out to be false or misleading over the course of the story.

EXAMPLE:

A narrator tells you at the beginning of the story that another character is out to get him, but in fact that character is nothing but kind to him throughout the story.

How to Choose Your Narration Style

Answer these questions to find the right narration style for a story:

> Do I want the narration to be objective or subjective?

> Would it be more interesting for the narrator to be untrustworthy?

> Would the story be clearer if the narrator is trustworthy?

> Do I want my narrator's thoughts and feelings to be a major part of the story? (Create a first-person narrator.)

> Do I want readers to identify strongly with the narrator? (Create a second-person narrator.)

> Do I want the freedom to explore different points of view? (Create a third-person narrator.)

CHARACTERS or ACTORS

Once you know where and when, you need to know who. If you're writing a nonfiction narrative, who are the actors in the story? If you are writing a fictional narrative, who are the characters in the story?

A character or actor is often introduced the moment the writer shows him or her doing something—or purposely not doing something. You don't have to tell the audience everything about a character or actor the first time he or she is introduced, but keep in mind that the audience doesn't know anything about a character unless you tell them that information. The audience often needs to know quite a bit about the characters to understand and enjoy the story.

EXAMPLE:

The author writes that the character does not play with other kids—why?

Sebastian Fizzlethwaite stared out the window of his family's small cottage. He couldn't run and play in the snow with the other kids, because he'd been born with a crooked leg. What nobody else in town knew, however, was that he'd also been born with something else: the power to fly.

The author uses a plot twist to hint that the boy is capable of extraordinary things.

The author tells you about the character by telling you what he can not do.

Character Development

If your characters aren't interesting, your story won't be very interesting. Nobody wants to read a story about a person who doesn't think about much, doesn't care about much, and sits around all day doing nothing. So it's important to create characters who are dynamic—they take action, change, learn, and grow.

We also want to have a full description of those characters. We don't just want to hear that a character is "resourceful." We would like to know exactly what that means: how they've been resourceful in the past, how they plan so they can be resourceful now—even who taught them how to be resourceful. Characters should be vivid—clearly described with enough well-chosen details that they begin to take on a life of their own in the mind of the reader.

How to Create a Character

Answer these questions to help start to create a dynamic character who is vivid in the reader's mind:

What does my character care about?

What does my character want out of life?

What do other people think about my character?

What does my character like?
What doesn't my character like?

What does my character look like?

What does my character sound like?

How is my character different from everyone else in my story?

Add a **T.A.D.D.** (Thoughts, Actions, Dialogue, and Description) to your character to flesh out your character and make him/her/it dynamic!

PLOT

← THE SEQUENCE OF EVENTS IN A STORY

A narrative is a narrative because it's about a story, not arguments or information. The story can have a real or imaginary plot.

A PLOT STRUCTURE is the way experiences are organized into a story. There are a few common plot structures:

Beginning •———→ End	Plots can begin at the beginning of the story and continue chronologically to the end.
Beginning ←———• End	Plots can begin at the end of the story and go back to the causes in the beginning.
Beginning ←——•——→ End	Plots can even begin in the middle of a story and move forward and backward in time.

No matter what, events need to unfold logically so that your readers have all the pieces they need to understand what happened—and what's happening! That doesn't mean everything has to be in chronological order, but it DOES mean that everything needs to fit together and be relevant to the story by the end.

How to Create a Plot

Answer these questions to create a solid plot, where all the events make sense in the reader's mind:

Where would it be most interesting for my story to begin?

Where do I want the story to end?

What is the conflict that needs to be resolved?

What change must happen in the plot?

What change must happen in the character?

What does the reader need to know to understand what's happening?

What would be good to keep hidden from the reader to build suspense?

When is the best time to reveal details you've hidden to build drama?

NARRATIVE TECHNIQUES

To develop characters or narrative experiences, you can use narrative technique such as:

> Dialogue, **which reports the things people say to each other**

EXAMPLE:

"I'm hungry," one of the kids outside of Sebastian's window said.

"So am I," said the girl in the green coat. "Everybody's hungry this winter. Nobody's been able to get down to the town in the valley for so long. But thinking about it won't make it better. Let's make another snow angel."

> Pacing, **which is the speed at which things happen**

FAST-PACE EXAMPLE:

The girl in the green coat lay down, waved her arms a few times in the fresh snow, and stood up, leaving the imprint of an angel in the fresh-packed white snow.

SLOW-PACE EXAMPLE:

The girl in the green coat lay down. For a long moment, she stared up at the blue sky, thinking of warmer days, when the hilltop, which was now covered with snow, had been covered with strawberries. The thought of it made her mouth water. Then the hunger in her belly made her eyes water.

After a minute, to distract herself, she spread her arms out in the unforgiving snow and waved them up and down at her sides.

She was so hungry that she wasn't sure if she had the strength to stand. But when the cold of the snow began to bite into the backs of her legs, she found her way to her feet and looked down at the image of the snow angel she had made in the fresh-packed white snow.

> **SENSORY**
> related to our senses

Description, which gives **SENSORY** information about characters, places, or experiences. In fact, a good way to describe a scene is to think of how it would be experienced through several of your senses.

How would it feel?
How would it look?
How would it sound?
How would it taste?
How would it smell?

← But make sure the senses are relevant to the moment you are describing. Otherwise it's a bunch of meaningless detail to wade through as a reader!

EXAMPLE:

Sebastian always waited until it was too *dark* **SIGHT!** for his mother to see anything before he allowed himself to float out of his bed and explore the *quiet* **SOUND!** house. But this time he didn't just explore the house. He flew quickly to the front door, opened it, and flew out into the *chilly* **TOUCH!** night. The *scent of the pines* **SMELL!** on the hilltop was strong, but he didn't linger to enjoy it for long. Instead, he dove down the hill, flying at top speed, heading for the city in the faraway valley and the good things he planned to bring back for his family and friends to eat. The piles of fruits and cakes were so clear in his imagination that he could almost taste the *sweet and juicy* **TASTE!** first bite.

Word Choice

Descriptive language should also be precise—which means choosing just the right word.

IMPRECISE EXAMPLE:

In the city, Sebastian filled his knapsack with a lot of food.

PRECISE EXAMPLE:

In the city, Sebastian filled his knapsack with sausages and mushrooms, candies and cheeses— so many that the bag strained at the seams.

CONCLUSION

If your story is well written, everyone will want to know what happens at the end. The reader wants a conclusion to the story. In a narrative, a conclusion needs to do two things:

Just like in argumentative and informative writing, you should use transitional phrases and signal words in narrative writing. Instead of signaling transitions between information or arguments, you can signal transitions in setting, experiences, and events.

1. **FOLLOW THE PLOT:**
What happens at the end needs to follow logically from the events of the story.

EXAMPLE:
If Sebastian has to fly down the mountain to get food for his hometown because there was no other way to get there, he can't take the train back. That doesn't make logical sense.

2. **REFLECT THE NARRATED EXPERIENCE:**
Characters should act in a way that is consistent with their previous actions and thoughts.

EXAMPLE:
If Sebastian hasn't been able to walk before, he shouldn't start walking at the end of the story for no reason. Or if Sebastian has been a genuinely nice guy for the whole story, he shouldn't suddenly turn mean.

Characters should be vivid and dynamic, which means they should grow during a story. However, a character shouldn't suddenly become something they weren't before without any explanation. That's not good narration....

But that doesn't mean there can't be a little surprise at the ending.

EXAMPLE:

After everyone else had eaten their fill, the girl with the green coat came over to Sebastian.

He had to admit to himself that he had hoped she might talk to him after he "found" the food and donated it to the village, even though he didn't know what he hoped would happen next.

"Sebastian," she said, pulling his rolling chair around to the side of the house, where nobody else could see them. "I have something to tell you."

Sebastian's heart soared. Was she going to confess that she loved him as much as he loved her? Maybe that was too much to hope. Anyway, he thought, the smile on her face was already reward enough.

But to his astonishment, she didn't do any of this.

Instead, as he watched, her green shoes lifted neatly from the snowy ground, until she was a foot above the earth.

Then two feet.

Then three.

"I can fly, too!" she said.

Like a shot, she disappeared above him into the clear blue sky.

1. What is another name for narrative?

2. What is another name for the perspective from which a story is told?

3. True or false: Try to use only one sense at a time when you are writing descriptive passages.

4. True or false: A story has to begin when the events of the story begin and continue until they end.

5. What do we call passages that quote what people or characters say when they talk with each other?

6. What do we mean when we say something is written in first person, second person, or third person? Define each.

7. What word describes the speed at which things happen in a story?

8. Where would you like to set a story? Write five details that describe the setting.

9. What kind of characters would you like to write about? Imagine three characters and describe what they want out of life and how they hope to get it.

10. Think about what would be the most interesting moment for your story to start. Then write the first page of the story, setting the scene and introducing your characters. Then, if you want, write the second, and the third, and . . .

CHECK YOUR ANSWERS

1. Story

2. Point of view

3. False

4. False

5. Dialogue

6. First-person narrators are characters in the story and tell the story from his/her/its point of view, using words like "I." Second-person narration tells the story as if it is happening to the reader, using words like "you" and "yours." Third-person narration can tell the story from multiple points of view and uses words like "he," "she," and "them."

7. Pacing

#8 through #10 have more than one correct answer.

8. Answers should vary—this is your own story to tell!

9. Answers should vary—this is your own story to tell!

10. Answers should vary—this is your own story to tell!